Falling Apart
and Other Fallacies

Stories of Survival and Recovery

Falling Apart
and Other Fallacies

Stories of Survival and Recovery

Pat H. Fulbright

Smyth & Helwys Publishing, Inc.
Macon, Georgia

ISBN 1-880837-27-7

Falling Apart and Other Fallacies:
Stories of Survival and Recovery

by Pat H. Fulbright

Copyright © 1993
Smyth & Helwys Publishing, Inc.
Macon, Georgia

The paper used in this publication meets the minimum require-
ments of American National Standard for Information Sciences—
Permanence of Paper for Printed Library Materials, ANSI
Z39.48–1984.

Library of Congress Cataloging-in-Publication data

Fulbright, Pat H., 1934–
Falling Apart and other fallacies ; stories of survival and
recovery / Pat H. Fulbright.
x+179 pp.   6x9" (15x23 cm.)
ISBN 1-880837-27-7 (acid-free paper)
1. Stress (Psychology)—Case studies. 2. Resilience (Personality
trait)—Case studies. 3. Mental health. I. Title.
RC455.4.S87F85 1993
155.9'3—dc20   93-14913

CIP

Contents

Preface

I saw him in a theme park. Across the front of his T-shirt, I read "SURVIVOR, WINTER OF '77." I chuckled to myself. The humor was that he looked as if he hadn't survived it but had been through some terrible destruction. He was an older man, stooped, haggard, and rumpled.

I remembered the winter. Ice and snow pelted the nation for weeks during January. Blizzards snarled traffic and closed businesses. Heavy snows and low temperatures gave millions of persons a bitter taste of winter in the midwest, northeast, and southeast. The Mississippi River in places was 100 percent ice-covered with 20 inches of ice. River traffic was grounded. In Wisconsin, temperatures fell to 60 degrees below zero.

The new governor of Missouri, Joseph P. Teasdale, was inaugurated on January 10 in an outside ceremony in Jefferson City, with a wind chill factor of 30 degrees below zero. He alternated holding his speech securely with one hand and putting his other hand into his overcoat pocket, while spectators simply sat there and froze into statue-like posture.

Through the years, I've met survivors of many things. With the help of others, many of us are learning to recover from even the most devastating blows that life can give us. Better still, we are learning to be reasonably happy through it all.

The human spirit is indomitable. There is something in us that says, "I don't want to die. I don't want to give up. I don't want this 'thing' to conquer me." There is an unyielding will to keep going, no matter how difficult the situation.

Over and over you'll see this will in the stories of this book. When I met Carmen, I discovered that she was (and is) recovering from her own alcoholism, a very painful divorce, and the addiction of one of her children. It can be done. It is best done with the help of trusted counselors, friends, family, and support groups. For many people, support groups have provided the strength they needed to endure.

Consider the following examples of courage and patient endurance.

•Actor Charles Durning spoke for us all when he said, upon receiving a Tony Award for his performance in *Cat on a Hot Tin*

Roof, "I don't deserve this, but I have arthritis and I don't deserve that either."[1] The truth is, most of us don't deserve the "slings and arrows of outrageous fortune" that sometimes plague us.[2]

•Another struggler said, "His earbones ached to hear a good peal of honest laughter."[3] He grew up in poverty. His mother died when he was nine. One of his sons died at age four and another son at age eleven. The man himself suffered much personal criticism in his lifetime. He was Abraham Lincoln.

•Others, too, survive with humor. Chauncey Vowiel was a long-time member of our church until his death several years ago. (I liked him as soon as I found out that he had actually played in John Philip Sousa's band.) Rumor says that once he was watching a very obese man being baptized by immersion in our church. He said quietly to the people sitting around him, "Head for the chandeliers, boys. She's going over!"

The thought of Chauncey—and others—swinging from the chandeliers while the church flooded has gotten me through many an emotional moment, including weddings and funerals. (We all have our own coping methods. It's an inherited trait in my family to cry easily. My Aunt Verla cried if you just looked at her.)

There's an even deeper meaning to Chauncey's wit. As we see the waters of adversity rising higher and higher around us, each of us attempts to grab onto something or someone for survival. We discover that, in order to survive, we must begin a process of recovery. Our encounter is not just survival, it is *growth*. We must ask ourselves, "How am I changing and becoming a better person?"

Connie did just that. She was rejected as a child and repeatedly beaten by one parent She mourned multiple family deaths within one year and was date-raped. She says:

> In the beginning of our recovery, we open the dungeon door marked "pain" just enough for us to glimpse the light of recovery shining from behind it. The first rule of door-pushing is: Never push alone. It can kill you. You need a moving team, a support team that will be there as you are making momentous changes in yourself. Never, ever push alone. Loving, compassionate friends, support groups, and a treasured counselor have shown me a kind of living that I never knew was possible. A "team approach" to recovery has pulled me through.[4]

Madeleine L'Engle says in her book, *Trailing Clouds of Glory*,

> We cannot be fully alive without courage, and courage does not exist where there are no obstacles to surmount, nothing to fear. . . . All through our lives we are called to be courageous. . . . We learn courage from each other, by seeing other people react to difficult and dangerous situations with courage, people we meet in real life, people we meet in story. Nowadays the people from whom we catch courage and openness and Naming are called role models. They used to be called heroes and heroines.[5]

In this book, you'll hear from executives, street people, the clergy, the addicted, the lost, the locked-up, "saints," "sinners," the battered, the betrayed, the abused, and even from children. You might be surprised to know who they are in real life. Certainly, they don't understand the "why's" of life but are determined to get through it. Though it isn't included here in every personal account, almost everyone spoke of a Higher Power and His help in their lives.

My deepest appreciation goes to those who have helped me "survive" the writing: Paul and Cathy Duke; Evelyn Shellhammer; Homer Hall; Nell Bishop; Susan Landrum; Jan, Betty, and Gay; and my ever-patient family.

The book is dedicated to the *real* writers—those who have shared their stories and, thus, relived their incredible pain. Much of their grief began in childhood. It is fairly certain that each of you will find yourself somewhere within these pages. May you rise from troubled waters to stand again on solid ground!

Pat H. Fulbright

Notes

[1]As cited in a sermon by Paul D. Duke.

[2]*Hamlet*, Act III, Scene 1.

[3]Paul Zall, *Abe Lincoln Laughing: Humorous Anecdotes from Original Sources by and about Lincoln* (Berkeley: University of California Press, 1982) 6.

[4]From a personal conversation. Used with permission.

[5]Madeline L'Engle, *Trailing Clouds of Glory* (Louisville: Westminster/John Knox Press, 1985) 42.

Chapter 1

Everyone's Dad Wears a Hat

Her name was Mrs. Brown, but she had red hair. I met her when I put an ad in the paper for my housecleaning services.

I arrived at her house every Friday morning at nine, looking very much the part and thinking I was *someone*. I left every Friday afternoon at one, realizing that I was *no one*. Mrs. Brown yelled at me, she yelled at Mr. Brown, and she yelled at the dog. I vacuumed too fast, I vacuumed too slowly.

I "resigned" when she told me that I could no longer empty the mop water in the toilet, the basement drain, or even in the yard. I was to take it 50 yards down the street and empty it into a culvert on the other side. It was just "too much." For months, my self-worth had been suffering at the hands of Mrs. Brown. And, without self-worth, we are nothing.

It was vastly different at Mr. Holly's, where I went to clean on Wednesdays. Such a nice man. He told me that I could use his magnificent stereo system and his collection of compact discs whenever I wanted. And I did! I blasted myself and the dogs almost out of the house. I was not the mopper, the duster, or the scrubber. I was an eagle flying gracefully over the canyon in the Grand Canyon Suite, or the reformed Eliza Doolitle in "My Fair Lady." I reached heights unknown and, when I left his house, I always felt good about myself.

We are born into this world with a certain amount of good self-regard. We say "Here I am, world. I deserve to be fed, changed, talked to, and cuddled. I'm going to cry until you meet my needs." But, somewhere along the way, some of us lose those first moments of feeling "I'm special." Our recovery from being knocked down is slow and painful.

The trick to maintaining self-value is to achieve it without falsely trying to place ourselves above other people (grandiosity, false pride). On the other hand, we may give it away by placing ourselves beneath others.

Dr. James L. Sullivan, who for many years was the president of the Baptist Sunday School Board, said,

> I never met a man I couldn't learn something from. There is a farmer who can plow a straight row and I can't. There is a woodsman who can fell a tree and make it fall at the exact spot where he wants it to. It matters not who he is, what he is, or where he lives. He is a potential teacher of mine. Therefore, I should respect all persons.[1]

Because of his feelings, Dr. Sullivan often left the executive suite to visit in the building with employees whose jobs were considered menial. He was a much-loved and respected man. He also gained knowledge because he was not too arrogant to respond to others, whom he could have considered beneath him. He helped individuals gain self-esteem rather than destroy it.

Dysfunctional Families

Among the great destroyers of personal worth and self-value is the dysfunctional family. Families that provide a supportive environment for their members and allow them to grow are "nurturing" families. Dysfunctional, or "troubled," families block the development of their members in some way. Most families are a little of both.

Examples of dysfunctional families are those in which there is mental illness, addiction, or abuse. According to recent media reports, an estimated six and one half million children or more, under the age of 18 years, live in American households with at least one alcoholic parent. There are also children who live with compulsive gamblers, sexaholics, debtors, and overeaters.

A child from such environments learns to judge himself severely. He *adapts* to the dysfunctional family merely to survive. He doesn't feel lovable, so he settles for feeling needed and outdoes himself in assuming responsibility for others. He thinks he has to "care for" his own unstable family, and often loses his childhood in the process.

"Gloria" was such a child. She found healing in adulthood.

My dad was a hardworking, honest, gentle man who became violent when he drank alcoholic beverages—even beer. His personality change made me realize in later years that he was an alcoholic. Thus, I am an adult child of an alcoholic and I come from a dysfunctional family.

When I was little, I recall looking out the window to watch daddy come home from work. If he stumbled or walked crooked, I wanted to run away. But, I became mesmerized by the action instead. Then the yelling and fighting would begin.

When I was about 10 years old, my father seemed to drink and fight more—mostly on paycheck days. Extremely unhappy with himself, he attempted suicide many times. Being Dad's firstborn and his "favorite" became a burden to me. When Mom couldn't talk Dad out of his suicidal ways, I was chosen to be the "rescuer."

My biggest enemy was fear. I remember my knees knocking as I walked out to Dad's workshop where he held a looped rope in his hands. He was going to hang himself from the rafters. I prayed God would help me and He did. Somehow my words managed to change Dad's mind. He meekly cried as I told him I loved him.

Several times I had to crawl through the bathroom window, turn off the gas water heater, and unlock the door so that my mother could pull Dad out of the gas-filled bathroom. His depression led him to seclude himself from those who loved him most.

I also remember going into a garage filled with carbon monoxide to open the heavy garage door. Then I ran to turn off the car's ignition. Dad lay under the car's exhaust pipe. His coloring was gray and he sputtered, coughed, and choked a lot from the deadly fumes. I gagged from the stench!

Since all of this bizarre behavior was the result of Dad's drinking bouts, I never told anyone about it. Not even my girl-friends knew of this awful problem. I kept my shameful secret inside me. Our family had an unwritten and unspoken code of silence that led to a repression of feelings.

As a child, I had recurring nightmares. I was given an awe-some responsibility for "life and death" matters when I was too young to handle them.

As an adult, I have sought counseling. A support group was recommended for me. I didn't go, though. But, I did read books that helped me better understand it all.

Today I'm still learning to let go of the past. I am allowing myself to heal and grow, taking one step at a time!

Parents may not realize the role *they* play in a child's severe judgement of self. Parents acquire their skills from prior generations.

People who come from dysfunctional families and did not "feel" anything as children will not "feel" anything as parents. Grief unshared becomes unfelt. It then becomes anger that deepens and is not processed. People filled with rage do not make good parents. Unexpressed anger can lead to obsessions and addictions in parents.

Perpetuation of Dysfunctional Survival Strategies

Dysfunctional parents use the only survival strategy they know—compensation. They may be protecting their own self-value. They dump their own feelings of "no worth" on the child, who doesn't have the skills to sort out what is happening. The parent is projecting exactly what he has grown up with—excessive negativism. The sickness perpetuates itself from generation to generation.

"Christine" is a victim of that perpetuation.

My name is "Christine" and I am a survivor of a dysfunctional family. The abuse I suffered as a child was less overt than physical or sexual abuse, more subtle and accepted by society, but just as insidious.

My father grew up during the depression in a small, rural town. His father, a carpenter, was unable to find work most of the time. The family was quite poor. My father was the baby of the family but, in terms of birth order, responded as if he were the oldest. He was made to take on chores and responsibilities that were beyond his years.

My grandfather was physically, verbally, and emotionally abusive, directing most of his rage and domination toward my father, since he was the only one of the children who would take it. My father was the abuser in my family. My mother became a victim like the rest of us—unable and unwilling to challenge his authoritarianism and abusive behavior.

As early as I can remember, I felt that God had made a mistake and put me on the wrong planet. My perception of reality and the reality I was living with my family were two separate entities that never overlapped, creating a sense of not belonging, or displacement. As a toddler, I developed asthma, which (as research now supports) was a response to a stressful environment. I suspect that my father's rage attacks, over-controlling and perfectionistic behavior, and domination were present even then.

One of my earliest memories is of one particular Sunday morning when our family was getting ready for church. Since I had finished dressing and was ready to go, my mother gave me permission to sit on the front porch steps until it was time to leave. My father decided that he would put the family in the car and drive off, pretending to leave me as a joke. Since the garage was in back of the house, I had no way of knowing that my family was leaving. When I saw them drive away, needless to say, I was frantic as I ran screaming and crying after the car. I can still remember my father's sadistic laughter as he stopped to let me in the car and the pleasure he appeared to receive by making fun of my feelings.

My father seemed to enjoy our pain. He purposely would not intervene to relieve it. Often, he watched from the sideline as we headed for disaster, laughing at us as we accidentally hurt ourselves or made mistakes that could have been prevented.

As an adolescent, I continued to be depressed. I had little confidence in myself. One incident, in particular, although there were many, reflects my father's inability to support my efforts as well as build self-esteem. I became aware that there was nothing I could do to make my father happy or to please him the day I brought home an honor grade in math. I was hoping that for once in my life he would be proud of me. My hopes were dashed, however, when I showed him my report card. His only response was to ask me why I had not gotten honor grades in my other subjects, while ignoring the honor in math.

Situations similar to this one continued all through my growing-up years. Either criticism or unconcern was my father's typical response. Praise and encouragement were never articulated or demonstrated in my house.

After high school graduation, I went away to college mainly to get away from the oppressive presence of my father. My study skills and my ability to organize my time were not developed to a point of handling college demands. My confidence in my ability to perform was zero. In addition to all of that, I had an undiagnosed learning disability (L.D. was virtually unknown in the 1960s). Somehow, I managed to get by by the skin of my teeth for three years.

My lack of academic skills finally caught up with me, and I flunked out of school at the end of my junior year. Even though the college allowed me to return in the fall on probation, I knew I was not going to succeed in college. But, I could not imagine going back home. After I began the fall semester, I found out I was pregnant.

I really believe that at a subconscious level I allowed myself to become pregnant because my options were limited. I had no idea of what I wanted in terms of a career. I had no skills, and I had no confidence in my ability to take care of myself.

The resulting marriage was tolerable. In some respects, though, my husband was similar to my father. His ability to intimidate emotionally and to communicate on a one-to-one basis was similar to my father's. However, he was not verbally abusive. Thus, an atmosphere existed in which I began to develop confidence in myself.

I finished my under-graduate degree. I started teaching and completed my master's degree. I read every self-help book I could get my hands on. As I read, I began to find bits and pieces of information that helped explain my struggle. On the other hand, not until professionals in the field of chemical addiction began writing about addictive and co-dependent behaviors was I able to put together all the pieces of my problem and see it as a meaningful whole.

Survival has been a difficult process for me. There have been many ups and downs even with professional help. I have been in group and individual counseling, which I continue with today. I find that it is important to have someone I can trust, someone who will accept me no matter where I am emotionally.

A "trust person" can be a sibling who has lived through the same abuse, a friend who has been in a similar experience, a therapist or counselor, or a person who is unusually accepting and a good listener. For those of us from dysfunctional families, it is critical to share our stories with people who will hear us and validate our feelings.

Also, a support group meeting on a regular basis will increase our awareness and knowledge, expose us to other people who are struggling with the same abuse issues, and offer encouragement. Another technique, which has helped me to survive, has been learning to value some of my dysfunctional behaviors. For example, my persistence and over-developed sense of responsibility have helped me to complete my education and further my career as well as pursue my search for peace up to this day.

"Lost Children"

Like "Christine," a "lost" child in the family system may actually attempt to fulfill the negative messages she receives about herself! Self-esteem is self-value, and "lost" children don't have any. With no one to deny it, little children soak in and believe the criticisms of their parents. These children lose all ability to express their feelings and lack trust in family members. They feel incapable of being loved, asking, "What could anyone see in me?"

"Lost" children are also plagued by repressed feelings—feelings that are part of their subconscious minds. At some point, those feelings emerge to be more devastating than ever.

One adult child of an alcoholic shares her distress.

Because of some deep depression, I went into therapy. It was a "balm" to my soul. I discovered so many things about myself. For instance, I learned why I was always depressed during the Christmas season. In my childhood, my dad was always drunk at Christmas. It became a time to fear and dread. I repressed those feelings then. But, unknown to me, they carried over into my adult life. Every year I relived those painful times kept deep within me at a place I didn't know. Once I realized that, I was able to shake off the shackles of sadness. Christmas is now my favorite time of the year.

"Joe" also blocked out the painful memories.

"Why don't you remember?" my wife Karen asked me repeatedly throughout the first two decades of our marriage. I was denying my past. Repeatedly I responded, "I just don't remember." Then, I would drop the subject, at least until Karen and I again discussed our childhoods. Let me tell you about my situation.

My mother was 17 years of age when I was born. Essentially, she had married my father to escape a rather primitive home environment. I am sure Mom loved Dad - he was a dashing high school football player with a pickup truck. What more did a beautiful, high school freshman need? It was enough chemistry for a wedding, but not for a marriage.

Even after their divorce, my parents did not learn their lessons well. Mom entered into about eight marriages. Some of her husbands had no business being stepfathers to my brother and me. She slipped in and out of alcoholism until 1990 when she died from lung cancer because of a lifetime of smoking. Dad is in his fourth marriage. He never has really become an adult in maturity. His negative condition is always someone else's fault.

My childhood and adolescence were filled with insecurity and sometimes terror—from physical and emotional abuse that came from step-parents and even emotional neglect from my Mom and Dad. My parents had no time or energy left for my brother and me because of having to deal with their many problems.

I developed my survival skills early. I became independent and determined to be responsible for myself alone. I consciously refused to remember painful incidents in my life. I put my hope and energy into a better tomorrow. During my high school years, I moved away from Mom and her third husband to live with my paternal grandparents. They became my emotional parents, particularly my grandmother.

In college, I was fortunate to marry Karen. My Christian faith and my marriage have become two very stabilizing influences in my life. Yet, my recovery was incomplete. I needed to remember.

After returning from Mom's funeral, I sat down with Karen and chronologically reviewed my life, attempting to remember the pain as well as the joy. I am also forgiving my parents and accepting my past. The good, the bad, and the ugly have all shaped me.

I am learning to move from independence to interdependence. However, much of this intentional transition did not begin to occur until I was 40 or 50 years of age. By that time, I had the necessary distance from my past and enough experience to reflect upon my dysfunctionalism. Sometimes these things cannot be rushed; they come when we can handle them as good stewards of memory.

Survival is not enough. To excel is what counts. Just recently three truths of immense value were revealed to me:

•Children are shaped by their vision of the future.

•Family background does not have to be an indicator of success.

• All who survive have something to do in their future.

A child who feels lost and abandoned in the family system feels no support for his worth. He will go to great lengths to please a parent so that he won't be abandoned, either physically or emotionally.

One mother shares what she sees and fears the addiction of her spouse and their dysfunctional home are doing to her children.

Naturally, our entire family is affected. Our eight-year-old has been through two ten-week childrens' programs at aftercare. The sole purpose of these programs is to get the child in touch with her feelings. She has been helped, though she still suffers from low self-esteem. She has some difficulty with friendships, motivation, attitude, and family relationships. My behavior is part of her problem. I'm trying to find help for her through a latency program for children of alcoholics. My husband denies that she needs any help.

Her three-year-old sister is the bright spot of our family. This child's disposition and attitude are definite pluses (most of the time), but I suspect she too is getting sick. She is quick to say 'I'm sorry' when anything goes wrong.

Shame-based Identity

If, as a child, you learned to feel ashamed of the behavior of someone else in the family, you did not have high self-esteem. If you deal with shame long enough, you may have a shame-based identity. This means that you are ashamed of your identity. A child learns to believe "something is wrong with this family; therefore, I am ashamed of who I am."

"Beverly" says, "I didn't know until recently about shame-based identity, but as a child I knew all about shame." She describes her experience with shame this way.

> When I was about ten years old, a neighborhood playmate asked me, "Why doesn't your dad wear a hat? Everyone's dad wears a hat." Her father was a successful businessman. Not only did my father not wear a hat, he was an alcoholic who never worked while my mother supported us. He lived in the basement most of the time. I prayed that my playmate/friend didn't know that about my dad. It was shame for me. After private therapy and years of support groups, I can put that painful memory behind me.

The shame is deep. You may try to hide it, but it is there nonetheless. When you feel shame, you work overly hard to succeed; you become a perfectionist. Victims of dysfunctional families must learn to *enjoy*. One adult said, "I could never *enjoy* my successes. There was always this feeling that I don't deserve to be happy and to express joy."

"Bob's" problems, too, began in childhood. But he needed to understand his damaged emotions as an adult child of an alcoholic. Bob describes his experience.

> I was born into an alcoholic, dysfunctional family with three brothers and sisters. Between the four of us, we have 12 children. All of us suffer from the effects of the disease of chemical dependency.
>
> My father and several of my uncles worked in a brewery. Our family outings always included the abuse of alcohol. One uncle drank himself to death. Another was killed while driving drunk. Accidents and other dysfunctional behavior seemed a normal way of life.
>
> I must say that my dad was the most moderate drinker of them all. My mother and father did show us some good values and ethics. My parents were basically good people. They were

raised similarly. I know there was some emotional and physical abuse in their childhoods. As children, we knew they loved us, but it was not expressed very openly. My sisters, brothers, and I married people with similar dysfunctional backgrounds, which, unfortunately, is normally what happens.

As an adult, I became a workaholic with low self-esteem. I stayed away from drinking because I had seen firsthand what it could do to a person. Instead, I used hunting as an addictive high. I was happiest when I was out in the woods. I went into counseling to clarify, locate, or discover any damaged emotions that I might have and to get a better understanding of the effects of being an adult child of alcoholism. I reorganized myself, set my priorities and goals, and received encouragement in the steps I was taking.

"Sadie" also faced emotional neglect in an impaired family. Ensuing problems confronted her in adulthood. She has survived painful memories and destructive emotions.

My family was rather strung out in age—almost as if there were two families. One family of children was almost grown when the others were brought into the world. Somehow a bridge was never built between the older and the younger members of the family. This was only one of the situations that made my family members' distance from each other more apparent.

The older children had the privilege of college and left home at appropriate times to make their own way. During the childhood years of the two younger children, our father became ill with tuberculosis. He was in a sanitarium away from the family for parts of five years.

Our family became centered on the crisis of our father's illness. The adolescent needs and development of the children were less important. Our father had always been negative and tyrannically sought to control all thinking, being, and doing within the family. His temperament became more and more negative and critical during his long years of illness. Much scapegoating and a veil of secrecy surrounded intra-family communication.

I was the youngest daughter and the family "hero." I was very careful not to disgrace the family. From all of my family's verbal and nonverbal communication, I felt a great deal of pressure to "do right." Out of this situation, my brothers, my sister, and I became dysfunctional. We were unable to get in touch with our feelings. Each of us became a controller. Estrangement dominated all our relationships.

My brothers turned to anger and withdrawal with alcohol. Their destructive patterns of behavior killed both of them in middle age. With the help of a counselor and a twelve-step support group, I began to internalize a need to detach in order to get out of the same destructive patterns. The twelve-step program focused on healing and health. The strength of the group was in providing the safety in which its members face their past.

Being emotionally safe enough to share is a treasured place—a new place with endless possibilities for growth. Learning to tell my story has begun a therapeutic journey for me.

Most of us are searching for ways to overcome the dilemmas of our childhood. Many of us know failure and emptiness. We have learned not to trust. Sometimes we have suffered irreversible emotional losses from our early years. Subsequently, we are unable, in our adult lives, to have healthy and fulfilling relationships. "Time" is not likely to heal us from a painful childhood. We must take steps to do that.

"Ugly Ducklings"

In the fairy tale, *The Ugly Duckling*, when the last egg cracked, out came the biggest and ugliest duckling the world had ever seen. When the new brood first went into the duckyard, a duck flew at the ugly one at once and said: "He is ungainly and queer. He must be whacked." To which the mother duck replied, "He is not handsome, but he is a thorough good creature. I think he will improve as he goes on."

The poor duckling was at his wit's end and did not know which way to turn. He was in despair because he was so ugly and the butt of the duckyard. The ducks bit him, the hens pecked him, and the girl who fed them kicked him aside. All he wanted was permission to lie among the rushes and drink a little of the marsh water.

One evening, a flock of beautiful large birds appeared out of the bushes. The duckling had never seen anything so beautiful. They were dazzlingly white with long, wavy necks. They were swans.

He could not forget those beautiful birds. How could it occur to him even to *wish* to be such a marvel of beauty? So, he flew into the water and swam towards the stately swans; they saw him and darted towards him with ruffled feathers.

"Kill me, oh kill me!" said the poor creature.

But what did he see reflected in the transparent water? He saw below him his own image. He was no longer a clumsy, dark-grey bird, ugly and ungainly. He was, himself, a swan!

To which the teller of the story adds: "It does not matter in the least having been born in a duckyard, if only you come out of a swan's egg!" What a powerful lesson for those who struggle with self-affirmation![2]

Consider again what self-esteem can do:

A 92-year-old priest . . . was venerated by everybody in town for his holiness. He was also a member of the Rotary Club. Every time the club met, he would be there, always on time and always seated in his favorite spot in a corner of the room.

One day the priest disappeared. It was as if he had vanished into thin air. The townsfolk searched all over and could find no trace of him. But the following month, when the Rotary club met, he was there as usual sitting in his corner.

"Father," everyone cried, "where have you been?" "I just served a thirty-day sentence in prison." "In prison," they cried. "Father, you couldn't hurt a fly. What happened?"

"It's a long story," said the priest, "but briefly, this is what happened. I bought myself a train ticket to go into the city. I was standing on the platform waiting for the train to arrive when this stunningly beautiful girl appears on the arm of a policeman. She looked at me, turned to the cop and said, 'He did it. I'm certain he's the one who did it.' Well, to tell you the truth, I was so flattered, I pleaded guilty.[3]

Notes

[1]From a personal interview. Used with permission.

[2]*Seven Tales by H. C. Anderson,* trans. Eva LeGalliene (New York: Harper & Row, 1959) 63.

[3]Anthony DeMello, *Taking Flight: A Book of Story Meditations* (New York: Doubleday, 1988) 105.

Chapter 2

No One Ever
Sang Me a Lullaby

In a sense, all the people you will meet in this chapter have felt betrayed. Dealing with betrayal is never easy, whether it be from friend, family, or foe. In betrayal, we are wounded. And "it takes the slow surgery of God to take out the arrow." [1]

Anger pervades betrayal/abuse. The victim should deal with this anger, get it out into the open, and then *put it to rest.* Most of us do exactly the opposite—we hide our anger inside us, learn to hate and resent, and get sicker. Eventually every action of the injurious person, regardless of how small and insignificant, offends us. Support groups have enabled many of us to deal with our anger by realizing we are not the only offended ones.

Women seem to have particular problems in feeling worthy and not feeling victimized. J. D. Goodchilds has stated:

> The language of co-dependency is just a modern way of explaining problems that women have had for decades, especially low self-worth and the role requirement to care for, and take care of, others.
>
> Women have been raised all their lives to put men first, to take care of everyone else in their lives, to marry the "Right Person" and happily take on the role of "Assistant Person." Thus, later they are surprised to discover that all this subordination of their personalities, abilities and needs carries a psychological price. [2]

Marital betrayal/abuse ranges from mild to severe—from abuses of the spirit to insults to life and limb. "Carrie" writes of her own "crushed spirit" and how she overcame it.

> I'm not sure when the harsh treatment actually began because it was so subtle. I think soon after the marriage ceremony. I had seen him as a kind, caring, and gentle man. That's why I married him. At first I thought I was imagining things, but there were little innuendos. My husband made little remarks, which I knew

no one else would understand, but that I felt were directed right to me. Some of his criticisms were not so subtle. Every day I felt him chipping away a little more at my self-esteem. Finally, I began to feel so unworthy.

In the early years of the marriage, I cried privately. Some days I could not function, so great was the pain I felt. Other days I was depressed. I loved my husband, but I would not, could not, believe he loved me. It wasn't as if he didn't understand how I felt. We talked about it many times. I suggested counseling for a "troubled marriage." He didn't want it.

Had someone in the past hurt him deeply? I wondered if that's why he wanted to "get back at me." With passing years, it seemed that he became more selfish, and with it, more mistreatment of me. He was condemning of me and of the children. Nevertheless, I tried to help the children have respect for him. Isn't that what a mother is supposed to do?

He never hit me, but he might as well have. I felt "knocked down." He compared me to other women, to his family. I didn't listen to him, he said, the way his brothers and sisters did. I didn't especially want to.

As the years went by, I stopped crying. My hurt, my pain, turned to anger and, worse, to hatred. With that, came my harsh words to him. I now had a new problem with which to deal. I had to try to pretend I didn't hate him. I began to have health problems because of the anger I suppressed.

All the while, I felt I had to keep it all a secret. To whom could I talk? Who would believe me? He was intelligent, capable, respected in the community. It was at home that I saw his unbelievable arrogance.

A friend, who knew of other problems in my life, suggested that I go to a support group meeting. As I listened to other stories of pain, I knew I was not alone. For some people there, it wasn't a spouse who had caused their pain and feelings of non-self-worth, but a parent, or a child, or a sibling. Those destroyers of self-value knew just when to gouge us, exactly how to apply the pressure to hurt us where it hurt the most. They knew how to put unrelenting guilt on us.

Gradually I began to see how really sick the sickness in my marriage was. I found friendship and love at the meetings, and a sincere caring for me. Even the way the people in the group said my name showed a respect I wasn't used to receiving. I have learned that I have a right to be angry and that anger is not a "sin." It is in trying to get revenge myself that I am wrong. My feelings about myself are getting better every day. I'm learning that I am a precious person and a child of God. I am a worthwhile person who can love myself unconditionally.

I help myself by continuing to go to the support group meetings. I know that I can't change my husband, but I can change *me*. Sometimes now I can even smile when the insults come, knowing how far I've come.

Physical Abuse

Some marital injury is much more severe, as "Nancy" attests.

He didn't mean to do it. Or so he said. My husband was a good person—kind, honest, ethical. He was nice looking and congenial. At least, he was good most of the time. His abuse started early on in our 27-year marriage. I loved him so—I still do. I was shocked to insensibility when he struck me. I had always thought alcohol caused mood swings and violent behavior, but he did not drink. So it was extremely difficult for me to comprehend a dramatic shift that changed from an easy-going, mild-mannered gentleman into a brutal assailant.

At first, I blamed myself somewhat, wondering what I could have done to set off his explosion. Sometimes, an argument was over money or some imagined insult. He was so unpredictable that he even hit me for not looking up when he spoke or for some other perceived slight. He was always sorry for what he had done, saying he didn't mean to do it and he didn't know what came over him and all that. I believed him, I guess because I wanted to so badly.

Everything I have read about battered wives places the blame on the abusee, stating that the victim is guilty, even sick, sick, sick to tolerate abuse. Though I knew he shouldn't hit me and I knew I should not allow it, I thought my case was different.

For one thing, I didn't believe in divorce. I considered it a result of failure that violated God's laws.

One can make a marriage work, I thought. Turn on the charm, baby him, wait on him, seek his advice, smother him with love, assure him how marvelous he is, initiate thrilling sex, be nice, be sweet, be forgiving. Praise him, love him, pet him. He'll be better. Maybe he *can't* help it.

In spite of the bad episodes, our years together were actually good. I always tried to make our home fun, secure, and creative. We had lots of good times and adored our daughter. My husband was good to my mother and to our extended family from whom I hid the ugly truth. I thought every abusive event would be the last. I did my best to accentuate the positive. When he was good, he was very, very good.

I remember that during some of the hard times when my husband had either screamed at me or hit me, I fought back silently. When I set the table for a meal, I would give him a fork with a bent tine. Such revenge! Of course, he didn't even know of this evil act on my part, but it gave me a smile. As I folded the napkin and placed a fork in it with a slight dent, I would think "Take that!"

How did I cope? My Christian faith nurtured and sustained me during painful times. Interestingly, when I prayed earnestly for guidance, strength, courage, and wisdom to do the right thing, sometimes it seemed as though the prayers were answered in unusual ways. I took courage even when the bad times came again, knowing God was hearing my prayers.

But the real solutions and answers came when my prayers became altogether desperate: "Lord, I've done all I know to do. I don't even know what to ask for or how to pray. Help. There you are and here I am. Help me!"

In some inexplicable way, this prayer of total submission brought me a peace I needed. Things got better for awhile. Then, when one of my husband's attacks was aimed at our young daughter, I knew it was time to make a change. It was time to get a divorce. My husband begged me to stay. He would never do it again. I was a wonderful wife, he said, declaring that he couldn't live without me. It was awful.

Divorce is mind-boggling. There aren't any soothing words to describe such horror. Fortunately, we did not have to go to court. Nevertheless, the procedure of separating is bloody torture. After the divorce, when my daughter heard someone refer to a broken home, she said, "Our home isn't broken, it's fixed." Well said!

Members of my support group convinced me of their continuing love. Friends were true, commenting on a necklace or blouse or something just to make eye contact. I'm better now. Not healed, but better. Does one ever heal from parting with the only one ever loved?

God has blessed me in multiple patterns. I feel like a widow, rather than a *divorcee*. What a loathsome word. Somehow I remember the wonderful times, not the bad, which is healing, I suppose. Our daughter is doing fine. I am, too.

Those of us who feel misused, like Nancy, may have been treated by others as though we had few or no rights. Exerting some independence can have a very healing effect on the bruised psyche.

Child Abuse

The most helpless victims of betrayal are the very young. Terry Madison has written,

It is tough growing up in any culture. Childhood is such a vulnerable time. Bones and egos are fragile. Those who should care for and protect children are often those who abuse and take advantage of the young. Sometimes it is family members who betray them; sometimes strangers.[3]

If we could hear a child on the inside, Madison suggests that she or he might be saying:

I am tomorrow's adult. How I am treated today will influence how I treat others when I grow up. What I see today will affect how I view my world tomorrow. The emotional pain and trauma I endure now will scar me for a lifetime. The inequities I suffer in my youth will be addressed when I get older. The threat to my life and limb by those in authority will be burned forever into my memory. The tragic loss of my innocence through the greed and hatred of adults will warp my values forever. The person I become will be profoundly affected by what I see, hear, feel, and experience as a child. Someday, should I live that long, I will become an adult. You may wish then that you'd done better by me now.[4]

With the shock of mistreatment comes powerlessness. A physically and emotionally abused child begins to feel ashamed and to say, "It's all my fault that this happened." A shame-based identity leads us to feel that we are not good enough, we are defective in some way.

Childhood is also a time of unquestionable trust. But when victimization comes, a child says, "I won't trust anyone, anymore." If the victimizer is a parent, the child may also blame the other parent who didn't do anything about it. In addition, he may fear to express anger toward someone who is much bigger than he is.

"Laura F.'s" story is a descriptive example of childhood betrayal and recovery.

> At the age of 20, I graduated from college *cum laude* with a Bachelor of Arts degree in art. Three weeks later I got married and moved to a big city.
>
> After living a few months with my husband, whose childhood was so "normal" he could have been Beaver Cleaver's next-door neighbor, I began to realize that my parents were *not nice* to their only child. Within a few months I changed my mind. Not only were they *not nice*; they were just plain mean. A few years later, an incident unlocked the door to my confused feelings.
>
> While I was pregnant with our second child, the doctor put me on complete bedrest. At the same time, my husband's company went on strike. He was sent out of town to work 12-hour days. I was left at home alone with our three-year-old son. I called my mother to stay with us. "Attilla the Hun" would have probably been more help.
>
> My mother arrived and immediately began to complain. She said her knees were giving her trouble and she just couldn't climb the stairs in our two-story house. So, each morning, for three days, I did what the doctor told me not to do. I went downstairs so my mother would only have to walk to our family room to bring me food or drink. It was an imposition on her to have to get up during commercial breaks on the television to get something as silly as a soda and a sandwich for her daughter.
>
> After my mother had been with me for three days, my little son came into my bedroom at 11:00 A. M. He woke me up and said, "Mommy I'm hungry and Grandma hasn't fed me any breakfast." Needless to say, I was upset.
>
> "Okay dear, I will get you something to eat," I replied. But before I could even get up, my son continued. "And, Mommy,

can you give me a bath? I don't smell good. I haven't had a bath since Daddy left." Now I wasn't upset; I was angry! I got up and began to see how my home had decayed in three days. The beds were unmade. That was something I, Miss Perfectionist, never allowed, though the beds in our home had never been made or sheets changed more than two or three times a year as I grew up.

Although I was supposed to be resting in bed, I made all three beds. Then I came downstairs. When I looked into my kitchen, my mouth fell open. No dishes had been put into the dishwasher since my husband left. My kitchen looked like the Wedding Room at Miss Havisham's house. I cleaned up the three-day mess. My mother didn't bother to get out of her easy chair in the family room or even acknowledge the fact that I was cleaning the kitchen.

As my son and I ate our brunch, my mother came into the kitchen. "Well," she said with disgust and defiance, "Why didn't anyone tell me they were hungry?" I had learned from twenty years of being slapped around, knocked down, and hit by this woman to hold my anger lest she attack me. My unborn child and my three-year-old could not endure one of her fits. So, I said nothing.

After lunch, I bathed my son and myself. I had an ultrasound scheduled at the hospital that afternoon. What the medical professionals found looked bad. They reached no clear conclusion, however, that the pregnancy should be aborted. When I arrived back home, I sank down on the sofa, feeling sick, lonely, and tired.

The words that came from my mother hit me harder than a slap in the face. "I knew that you would never be able to have another baby. I don't know why you are lying around. You should get up, start walking around, and get to work so that you can get rid of that dead baby. There's no reason to be lazy anymore because you're going to lose that baby."

Once again, I was ready to blow up, something I was never allowed to do as a child. I telephoned my husband. I told him to call his mother and see if she could come and stay with me. My husband called back in 30 tormenting minutes during which my mother continued to rave. My mother-in-law would gladly come. At that point in my life, the only difference I could see between June Cleaver and my mother-in-law was that my mother-in-law was a heavyset woman and didn't wear pearls.

I told my mother, "Mom, I think you are tired, and you need to go home and rest. My mother-in-law has agreed to come up with my husband this weekend and stay the week so you can have a break."

"I'll not have you telling me what to do. I AM YOUR MOTHER AND YOU DON'T TELL *ME* WHAT TO DO." Mother screamed at me as she had always screamed at me or my dad when she didn't like what we said or did.

I had a calm I had never had before. Once again, I said, "See, you are just tired or you wouldn't be so upset. I really think you need to go home." In the end, for the first time in my life, I won. The next morning she stomped out of our house.

My mother was right. I lost that baby and nearly died myself in the process. Amazingly, even with a revelation like I had that week, it still took me two more years to say, "I think I was abused as a child."

I went into therapy. For four months I unlocked memories of physical abuse, sexual misconduct in my family, and the fact that I was molested by a friend of the family. But the most revealing information was still to come.

One day I sat at the piano playing and singing a song that had become my theme song. As I sang the words "Somewhere over the rainbow, way up high, there's a land that I heard of once in a lullaby," I began to cry. I was an only child. No one had ever sung me a lullaby, kissed me goodnight, tucked me in bed, read me a bedtime story, left a nightlight on for me, or said a bedtime prayer with me.

Once the dam holding back my memories had been broken, a flood of other memories rushed over me during the next few days. No one had given me a bath, told me to brush my teeth, helped me with toilet training, or helped me get dressed. The list went on and on.

I had always been taught by my parents that if I expressed anger, I usually received a beating. So, I kept all my feelings inside. The road of remembering took me over two years. Along the way I learned to turn loose of my anger. I learned to give myself the care I hadn't received as a child. I even gave myself the one thing my parents never gave me—a party to celebrate the day I was born, *on* the day I was born.

I have pieced together the facts and found out that both my parents came from dysfunctional families. I know my mother is mentally ill, probably schizophrenic, and will never seek treatment. Most of all, though, I have come to know that no one can be my "mother" or my "father." I had to learn to be the parent to myself that I had been taught to be for my parents.

A brochure on child abuse warns:

There is no "typical" child abuser. They come from all economic, ethnic, and social groups. Most are "ordinary" people. Most know—even love—the children. Certain traits are common among people who abuse children:
   • Low self-esteem
   • Poor control over emotions
   • A history of being abused themselves
Stress is a major factor in child abuse. Too much stress can push even the strongest person to his or her emotional limits. Some common sources of stress include:
   • Financial troubles
   • Social isolation (no support network of friends or relatives)
   • Marital problems
   • Lack of knowledge about parenting
   • Illness
   • Abuse of alcohol and other drugs
   (drugs cripple a person's emotional control)[5]

Stanton Peele has described one particularly horrific account of child abuse.

The case of Joel Steinberg, who allegedly beat his "adopted" six-year-old daughter Lisa to death, is another middle-class instance of family violence that has gained tremendous public attention. Hedda Nussbaum, Steinberg's mate, testified for the prosecution that Steinberg had beaten her severely and that, in her resulting emotional state, she had allowed him to beat Lisa repeatedly and had been unable to call for help on the night the comatose Lisa lay dying.[6]

Multiple drug use has also been correlated with many forms of child victimization. Terry Hughes provides a vivid account of one drug-addicted abuser. Pat's children know the terrible trauma of having an addicted mother. Pat's friends saved her from drugs. Her crusade against drugs started when she was one year out of drug rehabilitation.

> I was watching how drug-addicted people were behaving with their children. Children were raising their parents, not parents raising their children. Parents didn't know what was going on. Kids were watching out for their moms, growing up too fast. Carmen, I remember when she was eight or nine years old—she's 12 now—she came up to me one day and said, "I want my momma back. You're not my momma. You're someone different."

Pat's oldest child, Antoinette, was handling all the bill-paying responsibilities by age 15. She was in charge of balancing the checkbook. Pat's income came from a succession of clerk or typist jobs, and drug dealing.

All of Pat's children were put in charge of shielding their mother from people who came to the door—sometimes peeking out from the curtains to see if they knew who was there, sometimes going dead quiet when the bills piled up. Mom warned them not to let anyone into the house.

Pat also disclosed: "My son, he was almost at the point of hating me. He started taking pictures of me when I was 'high' and showing them to me after I came down."

Death and fear sent Pat back to rehabilitation. She has stayed clean for almost two years. She works in a coin laundry. Now she provides a listening ear and is an encourager for other mothers who are drug abusers.[7]

On the other hand, Karen's children were *silent* victims of drug abuse. Her story was given in a report of the St. Louis Task Force on Drug Abuse and Child Abuse in Families.

> Karen, a crack cocaine user, has four children ranging in age from three months to four years. A nurse was visiting the family regularly because the infant was born addicted to cocaine.
>
> On a recent visit, the nurse discovered the children naked, smelling of urine and covered in feces. The electricity was turned off, and there was no food in the apartment. The mother was asleep and could not be aroused. The children and mother were seriously underfed. The children had sulphur powder in their hair, which indicated the house had been used to manufacture a great deal of crack cocaine.
>
> The children were removed and placed in foster care, and the mother began a drug rehabilitation program which she has suc-

cessfully completed. She has put on weight and is in good health. She lives with her sister while she looks for a job and an apartment for her family. She is afraid to return to her old place which is still a crack house. The infant and other children will remain in foster care until the mother is able to provide for them.[8]

Drug use by parents is blamed for a staggering increase in the number of children being placed in foster care. Some years ago, a crack house was busted in the inner city of St. Louis, Missouri. Viewers of television news casts were horrified to see 32 young children being taken out of the house. Most were so young they had to be carried out by police officers and social service workers. Fourteen adults were arrested in the same seizure.

Sexual Abuse of Children

As if physical and emotional abuse is not damaging enough, sometimes crimes against children become even more horrifying. Child sexual abuse affects people of all races, religions, and socio-economic backgrounds.

The different forms of sexual abuse affect children in adverse ways. For instance, incest is very damaging and traumatic for all involved. It can cause a variety of long-term emotional disturbances and sexual problems. Child pornography is often an introduction to prostitution. Sexual abuse can degrade and emotionally damage children. It may encourage adult abusers. A child who has been abused needs help, even if no symptoms of problems are evident immediately.

A grown man wrote of the pain of his childhood:

Divorce. Why did this have to happen? Did I do something to make Dad leave? Why could I never do things right for him? Then, Mom's heart attack. Was she going to die and leave me too? Money was scarce, so a "boarder" joined us. With him came months of molestation. "Tell your mother, and something bad could happen." Mercifully, the boarder left. Eventually we moved to a different part of town and life was easier. But the damage was done. My self-esteem was shot. I was an emotional wreck, first trying desperately to please, then in angry rebellion. It was a pattern I would follow for years.

Who are these betrayers of children, as well as others? Patrick Carnes has observed,

> Almost daily, newspapers across the country carry seamy accounts of sexual misbehavior. Congressmen, clergy, and professionals get the most press, but the addiction traps people of all pursuits—white collar workers, blue collar workers, and homemakers. Their sexual compulsiveness ruins their lives and careers. For many of these people, those who want to stop but cannot, it is an addiction which falls like a shadow over all those who are affected. It penetrates and influences every aspect of their lives. Often the addiction is handed down from generation to generation and becomes the family's best-kept secret. But the shadow deepens as the addictive behaviors escalate.[9]

The incidence of sexual abuse and misconduct is staggering. Consider these selected items:

• In New Orleans, two men organized a Boy Scout troop to provide themselves and wealthy homosexuals with sexual access to boys.

• In Winchester, Tennessee, an Episcopal priest who ran a farm for wayward boys, was convicted of several "crimes against nature." He forced his charges to participate in homosexual orgies and filmed them for customers across the country.

• In Louisville, Kentucky, a minister who ran a mission was caught trying to sell a young boy for sexual purposes for $6,000 worth of food stamps and $1,000 in cash. He also pleaded guilty to distributing child pornography.

• On November 14, 1990, Los Angeles Lakers basketball star James Worthy was arrested in Houston, Texas, and charged with soliciting a prostitute.

•On July 26, 1991, "Pee Wee" Herman, of films and children's television, was arrested in a Florida theater and charged with indecent exposure.

•In August of 1991, the horrifying story of Jeffrey Dahmer emerged. He admitted to killing, dismembering, and photographing eleven victims whose bodies were found throughout the apartment. Hard-core pornography and videos were found in great quantities throughout his home.

•Serial killer Ted Bundy, who confessed to killing as many as 23 women, recalled that, as a boy of 12 or 13, he began looking at pornography and detective magazines he found in garbage cans. He called pornography "an indispensable link in the chain of events." There came a time when pornography no longer satisfied him, and he began to be tempted to carry out his violent fantasies. Bundy warned that the nation is failing to recognize the dangers of pornography. "There is [sic] loose in their towns and communities people like me."[10]

Sexual addicts can recover. Treatment begins with an admission of personal powerlessness and unmanageability, in this case over lust. Treatment consists of first, stopping the undesirable sexual activity. The second step is "opening the channel" that consists of breaking down rationalization and denial. The patient is encouraged to "keep no secrets." Group therapy is often used. He or she is then encouraged to substitute a primary sexual relationship for illicit sexual behavior. Then he/she is taught relapse prevention. The client learns potentially dangerous situations and coping skills as well as how to facilitate interaction and communication with other adults. The family unit is treated intensively over four to six months. Two years of follow-up maintenance is essential. With treatment, addicts can learn that sex does not have to be deviant to be satisfying.

In chapter 3 you will see the effects of child sexual molestation and meet the survivors.

Parent Abuse

Other kinds of betrayal/abuse invade our lives. We hear often of many kinds of child abuse. But how does one recover from *parent abuse?*

Hear a father's story.

> A tremendous burden lifted off our shoulders when he left the house. Even when he was still very sick and very active as an alcoholic, the whole family had suffered so much that it was a relief to have him leave. It was so sad to realize that he was destroying himself out there. But it almost got to the point where what had to be done was for the survival of the family.
>
> Family members, even knowing that he was out there suffering and leading an agonizing life, weren't confronted with it daily. We weren't fighting daily. There wasn't the constant turmoil—phone calls at all hours of the night, the police, other drug users, or whatever. We used to get endless phone calls in which a caller would hangup if the right voice did not answer. There was peace in a sense that the real right-now problems disappeared.
>
> Of course, one problem kept looming up all the time. What can we do to help him? I think that unless people actually go through this, they cannot understand the agony and the hurt. We found that unless people suffered as we did, they couldn't understand a child leaving home. They just couldn't identify with that. It's almost like forsaking your own flesh and blood.[11]

That parent has identified what has become so true for many abused parents. Even though there is pain detaching from an addicted child, there is a peace and tranquility in the household that parents may not have known for some time. Those parents no longer feel abused. It is freedom from ensnarement. The mother of an addicted son speaks:

> He came to our house on Christmas Eve and knocked on the door and asked to come in. "I'll just sleep in the basement on the floor," he said, "if you'll let me in." It was cold and snowing.

Perhaps he thought that the holiday season would break down our determination. Or perhaps he thought that the cold weather would be a deterrent to our saying "No." But we stood firm, believing he would find some place to stay. We watched him walk away in the cold and the snow.

It was the hardest thing we have ever had to do in our lives. But we had gone over this a thousand times. He knew the steps to recovery and had been offered help. Our nerves were shattered, our emotions frayed, and we felt we couldn't go through it in our house again. We hadn't ceased to love; we had ceased to be able to survive his presence. Now, we knew some tranquility.

Betrayal and abuse may be mild or it may be severe. But it never leaves us unscarred, and some have taken positive steps to recover.

Notes

[1]From a sermon by Paul D. Duke, "The Long Walk of Forgiveness," delivered at the Kirkwood Baptist Church, 22 September 1991.

[2]J. D. Goodchilds, as cited by Carol Tavris, "Do Codependency Theories Explain Women's Unhappiness—or Exploit Their Insecurities?" *Vogue* (December 1989): 220.

[3]Terry Madison, *Childlife, The Magazine of World Vision*(Summer 1991): 3.

[4]Ibid.

[5]*About Preventing Child Abuse* (South Deerfield, MA: Channing L. Bete, Co., 1989) 4–7.

[6]Stanton Peele, *Diseasing of America: Addiction Treatment Out of Control* (New York: Lexington Books, 1989) 214.

[7]Terry Hughes, "I Worry about People, Ex-Addict Offers Hand to Others" *St. Louis Post Dispatch*, 20 August 1989.

[8]*Together We Can Win the Real War on Drugs. A Report on the St. Louis Task Force on Drug Abuse and Child Abuse in Families* (St. Louis:Citizen's for Missouri's Children, 1991) 10A.

[9]Patrick Carnes, *Out of the Shadows* (Minneapolis: Compcare Publishers, 1983) 139.

[10]"Bundy Claims Pornography, Alcohol Led to Murderous Lifestyle," *(Missouri) Word and Way*, 9 February 1989, 1.

[11]Phyliss York, David York, and Ted Wachtel, *Tough Love* (New York: Doubleday, 1982) 186.

Chapter 3

It Will Come Back and "Get You"!

Actress Roseanne Arnold, entertainer LaToya Jackson, talk-show host Oprah Winfrey, and former Miss America Marilyn Van Derbur Atler have made public statements about being sexually abused as children. Some suppressed (voluntarily concealed) the experience for many years. Others repressed (involuntary memory loss) the experience as a survival mechanism.

Sexual abuse victims both suppress and repress their pasts. The abuse is too painful for a child to cope with. He or she simply blots it out of his or her mind and pretends it isn't happening so it doesn't hurt. Or, the victims may have been so young when the abuse occurred that they were unable to form thoughts or feelings into words. Experts on the subject of sexual abuse in children say that repression is very common. Adult survivors may have absolutely no memories of the abuse or only incomplete ones. They may blank out details of events, but feelings—such as anger, fear, or pain—may bury themselves deep inside the victims.

To get into recovery, the survivor must have a very competent therapist, one who is knowledgeable also in child development. Psychological trauma returns. Often the facts are jumbled, like a puzzle unassembled, because they were seen through a child's eyes.

To share their stories, victims must get in a "safe" place where they can experience trust. As they speak, they may hold dolls or stuffed animals to help transport themselves back into childhood. In Jenny's story, which follows, you will notice that she speaks of "my kid." She is speaking of herself, her inner child of the past, as she relives the events.

In a "safe place," I listened to the stories you're going to read in this chapter. I was skeptical. As person after person recounted experiences, I realized that not only were they being truthful, the symptoms and effects of their experiences were the same. Now, hear the stories of these people and rejoice in their ongoing recovery.

"Jenny" says of her perpetrator:

"He took my puppy and chopped him up with a corn knife to prove to me 'not to tell or this will happen to you.'"

My abuse began when I was very young and continued definitely to age 16. I had a flashback that got me in touch with a very early incident. I went into hypnotherapy and pulled the incident out. The abuse was from my oldest brother. My next memory reached back to when I was five. A person—a very sick person —abused me in a cornfield. The abuse was very scary, very violent. A man took my puppy and chopped him up with a corn knife to prove to me 'not to tell or this will happen to you.'

At age five, my first day of school, I was molested while on the school bus. Then, when I was 12, my uncle, prior to his wedding, started abusing me. I was staying at his house, and the abuse went on for years. I had to run to hide a lot. I didn't sleep well at night. My aunt was oblivious to it. She didn't know what was going on. My uncle would come home drunk and seek me out. He also introduced me to alcohol. After I moved back home, my dad started abusing me. I was abused by my uncle, my brother, and my dad—all in the space of two weeks.

Q: You have flashbacks of what happened, is that correct? So then you go into therapy and the therapist helps you to remember?

A: Yes, as bad as being in therapy is, it's helping me to work through the incidents instead of being so terrified of them. In therapy, you get in touch with your inner child and let that child help you figure out what needs to happen to make it safe enough to go through the actual trauma again, the whole thing.

It is amazing how children take care of themselves during abuse. They dissociate, pass out, black out, or whatever it takes to get away from the abuse because it's so bad. Emotionally, it shuts you down.

Do you know what it's like to have all those memories and not feel anything about them? Nothing? When you finally do get in touch with your memories, you bounce back and forth from anger, to sadness, to crying.

When you do get in touch with all those feelings, it's over-whelming. If I wasn't in therapy, I'd probably self-destruct. For the very first time, I'm realizing what 'my kid' went through and how scary it must have been for her. I fought going into a hospital for two and a half years.

Before recovery, when I used to walk into a room, I would stop and check out the situation. I would blend into the conversation. I would just blend into the wall. I never disagreed with anyone. I gave myself away totally, not saving anything of myself. I didn't know any tactics of self-defense.

I used to sleep with my shoes on. I was 35, and I slept with my shoes on "cause you gotta be ready to go."

I've been self-destructing forever, hurting myself any which way you can think of, from banging myself against the wall to slicing my wrists. It comes from a sense of abandonment—nobody ever really wanted me; I'm not lovable.

I was also sexually abused by two other uncles and by friends whom my older sister brought into the house. I suffered physical and verbal abuse from my youngest brother.

After I married, my husband didn't realize the extent of my sexual abuse until I went into treatment. During Family Week, he discovered how bad it really was. We have two children, ages 18 and 15. They've suffered dearly through all this. Once when I came out of the hospital after having my stomach pumped, they cried and yelled at me, and I told them to go ahead. I knew the importance of allowing them to share their feelings. The experiences have affected my family terribly.

I can sit in a room and listen to people talk. If it gets too scary for me, though, I dissociate like crazy. Often people in group therapy ask me if I'm with them. They ask, "Where are you right now?"

Safe places are really important so those attempting survival can be together, especialy when we are in a crisis. The basis for a safe place is trust. We're getting help, we're getting better.

Through Jenny's story, we see that a family might have been involved in sexual abuse repeatedly for generations. Victims are constantly "running away," physically, emotionally, or mentally.

A psychological process known as "dissociation" leads to the victim's inability to recall the abuse. When someone disocciates, his mind feels temporarily separate, split off, from his body. An intensive dissociation can lead to multiple personality disorder, as seen in "Sue's" story, which follows.

Sue held a teddy bear as she spoke. She had cried out for help, but no one had responded.

"The boys are being mean to me. The boys are hurting me."

My first perpetrator was my maternal grandfather. (I just started having those memories about two months ago.) Then, my father got involved in it. Then, my mother's brother and my two brothers abused me.

My two brothers are both older than I am. They started abusing me probably between the ages of four and six. We lived in a new subdivision where there were a lot of new homes being built. I would go home with bruises and puncture wounds from where I was hit with boards with nails in them. I remember going in and telling my mom, "The boys are being mean to me. The boys are hurting me." My mother would call my brothers in and very jokingly say, "Now you boys know you're bigger than she is. Now you stop picking on her." They would all laugh and walk out, when, in essence, I was crying for help.

I learned very quickly not to say anything. They are not going to believe you. Because no one believed me, the abuse actually got worse. The boys knew then that they could do it. I would hear, "We told you not to say anything, so now we're going to do even worse things to you."

My brothers also started calling in their friends from the neighborhood. Friends were invited in to abuse me any way they wanted—it was usually physical and sexual. The abuse just kept building. More and more boys were invited to do what they wanted to do to me. At one point I was being gang raped by 10 to 15 boys at a time. One of my brothers stopped abusing me because he said that when he saw my face, he couldn't stand seeing the pain and the fear and the terrors.

My other brother went on to "pimp me out," in essence. He sold me. If he wanted a soda, he had one of his friends buy him a soda. Then, instead of paying the money back to the friend, he said "Here's my sister, you can use her any way you want to."

Years later my mother said she never knew anything about all that.

Q: "Does she know now?"

A: I told my parents what had gone on, and they said they believed me. The only question my father had was, "Did you ever consent willingly?" My mother said, "I just can't believe this happened because I would have known about it." That wasn't the case at all. My mother was in the home with us all day every day, except for a brief period of two or three months. She says she never saw anything, never suspected anything.

A lot of my abuse in the subdivision took place in what was called an "underground camp." The boys dug big holes and then dug tunnels from one hole to another. They brought in snakes, frogs, and things they knew I was terrified of. They taunted me with them. Animals were used in the sexual abuse from the time I was 10 or 11 and, if I didn't do what I was told, I was beaten or cut with knives. My clothing hid my wounds.

When I was 12, we moved to a rural area. I thought "Oh, thank God, I'm not going to be abused anymore, I'm away from all these people." I did not realize that the source of the abuse had moved with me—my brother. He started talking to the farm boys. Increasingly they abused me on the farm.

Eventually, the abuse became very ritualistic. Other girls and I were forced to watch them kill animals. There was chanting. There were pre-arranged or pre-written statements. You and I might call them prayers. There were songs. My memory is so poor on this because it is something new that just came up in the last few weeks.

The boys were very methodical when they were making sacrifices and doing some of the things to me. Animal sacrifices were done in the same order—almost like a well-rehearsed, very well-planned, thought-out ceremony. One of the "leaders" was my brother, who is three years older than I. I know there were some very young children there, but I don't know the purpose of their presence.

In the spring of 1991, I learned that I have a multiple personality disorder. I had huge chunks of lost time in memory, like years that I didn't remember. This is an indication of Multiple Personality Disorder. I was working with a psychologist (I've been in therapy off and on since I was 18 years old) and I said, "You know, it's like there are two me's—a good me and a bad me. This is the me that all the good things happen to, and this is the me that all the bad things happen to." That started this doctor thinking that maybe I had some kind of personality disorder.

I didn't remember anything about the abuse on any level until October of 1989. I had made 37 suicide attempts, all overdoses. Those were in my 20s and early 30s. I had moved out of my parents' house when I was 18. I married an extremely abusive person whom my family wanted me to marry. But, I got out of that relationship after 11 or 12 years and two children.

I entered a sexual trauma treatment program. I am now working with a therapist who is phenomenal in dealing with multiple personality disorder. Right now I'm not sure exactly how many "parts" I have. We're still finding new personalities, learning about new "alters." That's mainly where my memories come from—from these personalities, or "parts."

I have no knowledge at all of the ritualistic abuse. I have an alter, another personality who is 14 years old, one who holds all of those memories. Through contact with this personality (with the help of my therapist) I know now what happened then. I have to go back and remember and allow myself to feel the feelings and experience everything I didn't then. That's the way you get through this. You have to go back and do what you couldn't do before just because you were trying to survive it then.

Q: "So your mind just blocked it all out, is that correct?"

A: I had no memory of it at all, to speak of. That's pretty simplistic, but that's the way multiplicity is for me.

Q: "How did your therapist call forth these "parts?"

A: She would say "'Susie.' this is 'Carol.' You're in my office and I'd like to talk to you today. So, if you want to come out and talk to me, please feel free. 'Susie,' if you want to, come on out now.'" ("Susie" is my four-year-old "part." She draws pictures and takes them in—pictures of memories and things that she can't explain verbally because of her limited vocabulary). "Carol" would say," 'Sue' brought a picture, and I'd really like to talk about it.'" So then I would switch to the four year-old and discuss the picture or whatever else was going on. When "Carol" wanted to talk to me again, she said,"'Sue,' it's time for you to come back now, it's time for you to come out.'" As "Susie," I would act, think, and talk. For the most part, my mannerisms were very typical of a four-year-old child or an eleven-year-old, or whatever "part" was out.

At home, I may suddenly get my teddy bear and curl up in my bed. When that happens, my 16-year-old daughter usually comes in and says, "'Susie', do you want a cover?" She'll cover me up just like she would a four-year-old. She's also gotten down on the floor and read storybooks to me. She explains, "I just act like you're my baby sister. I think you're neat, I don't ever want you to go away." There are other parts about which she says, "No way do I want to be around this 'part.'"

My 14-year-old personality, who went through ritualistic abuse, does not like to be seen or talked to. She wants to be in total isolation because she feels that people can see how bad she is. When they see her badness, she thinks that gives them permission to do whatever they want to do to her. If she is alone, no one can hurt her.

My dad and I have always been extremely close. Not until several months ago did I know that he had abused me. That was really hard because, of my two parents, my father was the one who was more supportive of me than my mom.

To me, my personalities are very real people. I can touch them, hear them, and see them. I can share their pain, their happiness, whatever. I think a lot of my friends don't comprehend that these are real people to me.

I'd like to say to anyone who might be reading this who is a victim of sexual abuse: "Just tell and tell and keep telling until you find somebody to believe you." Keeping silent is the worst thing you can do. As victims, we're told, "Don't tell, don't make a noise, don't say a word." I am reliving the trauma, and it is healing.

A therapist explains:

The traumatic memories in a multiple personality disorder victim are encapsulated into another personality (alter). This protects the original person from the trauma. Memories that are split are not known to the original person. The purpose of alters is to keep the trauma secret from the original. Gradually, through expert therapy, the original and the alter become acquainted.

When the personality changes, the facial structure and expression change. The original *becomes* that alter for a time. The experiences are not just a memory. They are *relived* in the mind and body of the victim. Often an alter will hear the therapist but will speak to the therapist only through the original person, as he would through an interpreter.[1]

One adult victim spoke of "body memories."

You may feel excruciating pain in your body in the area where the abuse occurred. Then suddenly, the visual flashback comes and you *know* what that pain means. Or, you may not be feeling right and you don't know what those feelings are until the flashback occurs. When you reconnect yourself with that incident, it's overwhelming at times. You need support to get through it. One memory may go on for a week or longer. It is a building process. You are in emotional upheaval.

You work through all the trauma, and finally you're able to let go of it by forgiving and forgetting. If you don't finish that process, it will come back and "get you." You must heal from that trauma emotionally, spiritually, and physically. Until you go through the process, you don't rise above it, or forget it, or cease to be affected by it. It interferes with daily functioning.

This is how "Faith" explains it.

"My older sister had told my mom, 'Don't leave "Faith" with Dad alone!'"

I was the third child in the family. Four years after my birth, my little brother was born. From the age of seven, I knew that I had a problem. I recall my father sleeping in my bedroom. At the time, my father and mother were not getting along. I was placed with my older sister in the same bed in my mother's bedroom. I was a very disturbed child, in the sense that I walked and talked in my sleep.

I remember a night when I had to go to the bathroom. Mistakenly I got into the wrong bed. My father began fondling me. That memory is the first recall I had that something had happened to me. I was so afraid. I couldn't get away, and he wouldn't let me get away. I wanted to believe that he thought I was my mother. I don't recall being able to talk at the time because I was so scared.

After that, my father repeatedly molested me, usually when my mother went out to shop. Otherwise, she was always in the house. When my father molested me, my body would be there but my mind would leave my body for my sanity's sake. I could vacate the sensations and the feelings at that time.

My sister knew what was going on since I shared a room with her and she was seven years older. She told me that when our father was still using our bedroom, he would call me in the middle of the night, late at night. As a sleepwalker, I would obey him and walk into his bedroom. My mother knew that. She was in the bedroom we shared at the time, and she did nothing about it. So my sister had a lot of emotional pain. She felt powerless over the situation. She was trying to protect me. She asked me to please tell my mother what was going on.

I remember one day standing in front of the refrigerator and telling my mother that my father wouldn't leave me alone, that he was hurting me. I asked her to please make him stop. She acted as if my words were too absurd to require an answer. I felt that I wasn't wanted, that I wasn't believed, and that I wasn't important to her. She never showed me any understanding and compassion that I can remember. I asked my mother over and over to protect me from my father. It didn't happen.

The abuse continued until I was between 16 and 17 years old. By that time, it didn't happen very frequently because I had learned how to manipulate. When my mother was preparing to leave the house, I would phone people and either have them come over to my house or call my father to get him away. I manipulated either to get out of the house myself or to have someone come over so my father couldn't touch me.

Now I understand that the circumstances in which we live and the things that we recall are not unlike a black box in an airplane. We know that any airplane has a back-up system. In case of an accident, it has a black box in it that records what took place. As individuals, we also have black boxes. Our inner child holds our black box. These are the tapes that recall how we were treated (the importance and many significant parts of all the events that have happened to us). The inner child is a delicate piece of technology. Not unlike the black box, the child holds the pain, fear, and other feelings surrounding certain incidents.

By working through my black box and my inner child, I now know that I was pregnant with my father's child at the age of 11 and that my mother took me to have an abortion. I know where the doctor's office was. I remember when I was taken up those long steps to go to that doctor. I know also that my father came and picked up my mother and me after dark. I was told that I had a thyroid problem. The truth was that I was pregnant.

I feel my mother knew that it was my father's child. She knew when I was seven years old my father was molesting me. My older sister had told my mom, "Don't leave 'Faith' with Dad alone." Later, when I was in group therapy, my body started responding and I went into a flashback. In the flashback, I went through the process of having the abortion. When I go into a flashback, I am responding to the circumstances that existed at that time. I have no control. My body was responding to that abortion. Twice since then, I have had similar experiences. I know that my body (my black box), my inner child, was teaching me what I didn't want to accept. Acceptance to my family meant being well-respected in the community. Probably it was for that reason that we moved when I became pregnant.

When I was an adult, my doctor he told me that I had been pregnant and had a baby. I could not believe that any doctor would tell me such a thing. Obviously, I had not had a baby. I had no recall of having had a baby. He kept insisting that I had. That birth had been blocked out of my memory. Later, I found out that I had indeed had a baby. I found it hard to accept that I had been impregnated, that it was my father's child, that I had an abortion, and that all these things took place in my body *without my recall.* (My black box held the recall, but only recently did I discover the facts.)

My father has been dead for over 13 years. I tried to have a healthy mother-daughter relationship with my mother. To this day, she would like for me to take care of her. But she will not acknowledge what has happened to me, share with me anything about it, or let me know that she feels badly about it. It's just like it's my fantasy, like it never happened.

About eight years ago, I met her in another community, in another town. We went out for a lovely afternoon and dinner. We returned to the motel room we were sharing. She got out her crossword puzzle and began working on it, which is one of her greatest pastimes. She sat at the round table by a window propped with her pencil and puzzle. She told me to go ahead and say whatever I had to say to her while she worked the puzzle.

I tried to begin. I know now that I should never have attempted that discussion on my own. We needed a third party, an impartial person, to help us through this process. But, I tried. I wanted her understanding so badly. I wanted a mother after all those years. I already had three children and three grandchildren, but I wanted a mother-daughter relationship, something I had never had before. She told me to stop a minute. She shook her finger at me, called my name, and said "You know I love you." She could have been telling it to a dog. I had to flee that room. My mother and I don't have any kind of a relationship between us unless I keep my mouth shut and don't honestly acknowledge anything about myself. I can't do that anymore. (I cannot accept her unwillingness to acknowledge my existence as it was then).

I have been very angry with my mother. Recently I took a picture of my father, told him how I felt, and then burned it. I feel that I have worked through that anger with my father. Then, I knew that I wasn't finished in that session. I grabbed a piece of paper, wrote my mother's full name and her birthdate on it and burned it. It was like putting up a tombstone. Since then I have not had any problem with thinking about my parents. I think that I have put those feelings aside. Through my therapy, I have a new family, a group of people who have supported me. My new family is honest. My old family said, "Don't tell what you know."

As a result of all this, I do not have a satisfying relationship with my daughter, her three children, or my son and his two children. Yet my youngest son, who is at home with my husband, does talk to me and visit me from time to time. I have lost my own immediate family, but I know that things can change.

These are the facts. I have come to accept them. I have come to understand that what happened to me was not something that I caused, not something that I'm responsible for. I'm not a sick person. The way that I was able to cope was "not to cope" but to establish another identity.

Treatment for victims of incest consists of allowing the patient to revisit the event, preferably in the safety of the therapist's office, and to experience again the feelings of being victimized as a child.

"Laura" did that in the process of her recovery. She could not relate as a daughter to her abuser. She says solemnly,

"I hated my father. He died some years ago, but I hated him."

The best I can remember is that I was abused from the time of infancy on to age 8 or 10. My perpetrators were my two brothers and my father, I'm the last of five children. One of my memories of childhood is that, as a small child, I'd get myself dressed in the morning, fix myself a bowl of cereal, go outside and play all day, and come in at dark. I never played with anybody else, so I had a very vivid imagination. I created games. During this play I was abused one time. I was out in the corn crib when my brother came in. I thought, "Wait a minute, you're supposed to be working. You'd better not get caught. What's going on? What does he want?"

I have just started remembering the abuse. When I was in a college psychology class the teacher and students talked about the effects of incest. A light went on. I thought, "Gee, maybe this has affected *me*." Before that moment, it was a part of my history, but I never gave it an ounce of thought. It was buried in my subconscious. I only remembered one part of it. The rest of it is new knowledge to me. My mind had completely blocked it. At that time, I put it away again in a closet and didn't think about it until four years later when I told my sister.

I didn't really tell her. She had always told me how spoiled I was because I was the baby of the family. I got upset with her one night and I said, "You want to know how spoiled I was?" I hesitated. She said, "What are you going to tell me, that you were raped by your brothers? So what? So was I."

So I put it away again in the closet. In the meantime, my life was falling apart. Through my school years, I was described through school as an angry, closed person. I never had any close friends. I never talked about feelings or what was inside to anybody who really knew me. I had friends I partied with, but I never let anyone get real close.

In grade school, I was cold and very much a bully. I had to dominate every relationship. That continued through puberty.

In the fourth grade, I started journaling. I remember writing, "I know I'm not as good as other people. That's why I pretend to be tough." I was the toughest kid in the class. Nobody ever challenged me to a fight because they figured I'd beat them up. But inside, I was really scared.

I hated my father. He died some years ago, but I hated him. When he walked in the door, my stomach cramped and went into knots. I had ulcers by the time I was in seventh grade. My father was respected in the community. He belonged to all the upstanding organizations. He was a eucharistic minister in the church. After he died, I was trying to think of one conversation we had held, and I couldn't come up with it. I never knew what was in his head. I can't remember talking to him.

He kissed me one time in my life. That was the day I got married. He never once told me that he loved me. He was a workaholic who provided everything for our family, everything but *love*.

This is how my mother found out that I am an incest victim. A friend of mine told me that she is an incest survivor. I don't know what possessed me to confide to her that I am also. I was compelled to tell her. She got me into therapy with an outpatient therapist. Then I went into the hospital for treatment. My sister told my mother about the incest. They both came to the hospital. They pretended everything was fine. I got my sister out of the room and told my mother, "This is not going to work. We are not going to play games anymore." We finally talked. She said she was so sorry, that if she had known, she would have stopped it.

Later, I went to her house, and she didn't hear me come in. I heard her talking on the phone to one of my perpetrators—a brother. I heard her make comments like this: "I don't believe it, and even if it did happen, it happened over 20 years ago, and why talk about it?" I left her a note that said, "Mom, I finally know how you honestly feel about this. I hope that someday you gain the knowledge to deal with your feelings, but right now the only thing I have to say is 'I feel sorry for you.'" And I left.

Before I went into recovery, I was drinking every day to get drunk. I married a man I could dominate because I would not have someone like my father. Now, recovery is good. It's really good. No matter how rough it is at times, it has really changed my husband and me. Life is good. I talk to my husband and kids. I talk to my friends. I let people in. I share feelings and emotions like never before.

I have three children, all boys. The oldest one has been more affected by this than the younger ones. I've been in recovery for a year or so—half of my youngest son's life, I've been pretty healthy. But my oldest one is more introverted than the others. He doesn't show his feelings. I was never there for him. I tried to be. I tried to talk to him more than my parents had talked to me. But ultimately, I wasn't capable of it. When he would fall down and get hurt, for instance, I would dissociate from him. I could not be there for him. Many times he'd pick himself up, "lick his own wounds," and go on. He's been affected by that.

I'm hoping that, as I heal, my son and the rest of the family can heal. I'm focusing on my nuclear family. I'm focusing on the healthier parts of my life and the family and friends who support me in my recovery.

More and more, victims are speaking openly about their defilement. In telling her own story, the former Miss America of 1958, Marilyn Van Derbur Atler, says that, while being sexually violated by her father over many years, she dissociated into a day child and a night child. Her day child had no conscious knowledge of her night child. Her mind had long ago left her body.

In 1985, at age 48, she confronted her mother about the sexual violations. Her mother looked at her and said, "I don't believe you, it's your fantasy." Marilyn felt total rejection and despair. Her sister said, "She's not making up stories. I know because he did it to me, too."[2]

The worst thing that someone can say to a child abuse victim is "Forget it," or "I don't believe you." It can't be forgotten until it is processed.

Sexual abuse of children thrives in secrecy. *But what the perpetrators think is hidden forever is not hidden at all, except in the subconscious minds of the victims. That should make perpetrators tremble!*

As Marilyn Van Derbur Atler says: "Your child may be mute tonight, but someday, your child will speak your name!"[3]

Notes

[1]Susan L. Landrum. From a personal conversation. Used with permission
[2]Marilyn Van Derbur Atler, "Sexual Abuse. Break the Silence!" A lecture delivered in Sunset Hills, MO, 23 January, 1992.
[3]Ibid.

Chapter 4

Half of a
Chicken and Four Eggs

"I'm thinking of going to work in a church in Kirkwood, Missouri," said my minister/husband. I was less than thrilled. (I was happy in Tennessee).

"Where *is* Kirkwood," I asked. "And who in the world would want to live in Missouri?" (I didn't think of it as the midwest; I thought it was north. As a born and bred southerner, I had never wanted to live in the north.)

Furthermore, all I knew of Missouri was from pictures that I had seen of big houses with large front porches. I knew the song "Missouri Waltz."

Reluctantly, I agreed to go, with the understanding that, if I died there, my bones would be carried back down south. "I can live in a foreign land," I said, "but I don't want to be buried in one."

I have survived ten years in Missouri, and I love it. I found the big houses with the large front porches. I love the old train station in the heart of town with its tracks crossing the main street; and the open-air market where, in the fall, hundreds of pumpkins add just the right splash of color to the fruits and vegetables. It's a special treat to visit O. K. Hatchery Feed and Garden Store, where one can buy almost anything. There's even a Purina Feed Store with a checkerboard on the front and side. I won't forget the glow of the Christmas lights from the train station when it's snowing.

Who wouldn't be inspired by the bells of St. Peter's Catholic Church on a Sunday morning? Who wouldn't enjoy browsing in Kirkwood Hardware, where you don't have to show your driver's license to prove you *are* who you say you are? And, as for the people, they're the best anywhere. For me, Missouri has been a serendipity I didn't even deserve.

But often displacement is painful and not so easy to survive. Displacement can be many things: a move to another location, incarceration, abandonment and subsequent relocation, or even losing residence within one's own country.

Incarceration

Incarceration for crimes committed is a displacement from which it is not easy to recover. One writer describes it.

> No one can adequately describe the loneliness that prevails behind prison walls as well as the man who has experienced it. Let me give you some idea about how much loneliness can affect these men in prison. Through a correctional officer at the Tennessee State Prison, I learned of a man who seldom, if ever, received a letter or a visit from his family, even though his "loved ones" lived nearby.
>
> It embarrassed this inmate at mail call when others received letters but he received none. In order to alleviate his embarrassment, he wrote himself a letter and placed it inside his footlocker. Each evening, after mail call, he would take out the letter and read it, or pretend he was reading it, as though it was a letter he had received from home.
>
> Of course this is an extreme case of the effect of loneliness. But, it is an example of how loneliness can affect even a person who is surrounded by hundreds of other men.[1]

He goes on to observe:

> Those of us who have not experienced prison cannot have a true picture of the conditions that exist, cannot know what incarceration does to a man. The inmate is told when to eat, sleep, when and where to do everything. His life becomes the property of the state, and even the simple decision of when to use the bathroom can become a decision for the state to make for him.[2]

Hope for freedom keeps some prisoners from despairing. "Lo" says of his prison days:

> Knowing that no matter how long I'm here, I will eventually get out keeps me from going crazy. I'm suffering here. When I first came in, I had the fear that someone would hurt me. Now I think it's like my old neighborhood, but with a fence around it. Some-

times I run into my old friends, as well as enemies, on the campus.

Some are surviving by calling on all their resources. "Bill" has been incarcerated in prison many times. Charges against him include burglary, possession of marijuana, and sale of a controlled substance. He is now scheduled for parole after two years. This is how he describes his confinement.

Life in prison, has been very stressful. My family has stood beside me. I have one brother and two sisters. One of my sisters has always been there for me.

Drug treatment here has been a positive thing with me, a big plus. The behavior patterns I know now are positive ones. I'm working my program. The best thing is having a spiritual awakening. I no longer depend on myself but on God. I've survived prison because my family has supported me and because my friends and I in prison are a "family." We are all related because of our use of drugs.

"Rock" has found a similar strength to see him through.

Some days you laugh and smile. Some days you don't even smile. Holidays get me down, my mom's birthday, Christmas, and Thanksgiving. At those times, I stay to myself. No one knows what I'm thinking. I don't want to hear (the) things some people say. I might "snap" and get in trouble and be locked up in a worse place. A police sergeant writes letters to me that have been a good influence. They're positive letters.

I read my Bible and pray, and that's a worship time for me. I do this every day. I know that without God I wouldn't make it in here.

Immigration

Imprisonment can also come outside the walls of an institution. "Juanita" relates her moving story of displacement as an immigrant. Her English is imperfectly spoken, but her message is clear. To understand her story, though, you first need some historical background.

In 1958, a large-scale civil war broke out in Cuba. The forces of Fidel Castro gained control of the government. Castro became premier and dictator. In 1960, he seized all American-owned property in the country. The United States cut off almost all trade with Cuba and broke off diplomatic relations in January, 1961.

Conditions in Cuba became steadily worse. All activities were brought under state control. A secret police force was formed to control the people. More than 100,000 Cubans left the country, settling in Florida. In April, 1961, a band of Cuban exiles, aided by United States support, invaded Cuba at the Bay of Pigs located on Cuba's southern coast. The invasion was completely crushed. Castro aligned Cuba with the communist bloc. Food shortages plagued the Cuban people.

In November, 1965, the Castro government agreed to allow Cubans to leave the country. From 3,000 to 4,000 Cubans a month arrived on the shores of the United States. Skilled laborers and men eligible for military service, however, were not allowed to leave the country. Others who were detained were those who had nothing valuable to leave there in exchange for their freedom. Those who were left were prisoners who had no recourse but to live with the dictates of Fidel Castro and a communist government.

"Juanita Morejon," a Cuban missionary, lived in the city of Pedro Betancourt. On May 2, 1963, she wrote to friends in the United States: "Yesterday was a sorrow day. Some young men from here were sentenced to death. It make me sick." Friends sent packages of clothing and medicines to her. The packages arrived three months after the mailing date. On April 16, 1964, she wrote, "I get one pound of meat every month, half of a chicken each month, and four eggs. Maybe you find a kind of pill that help me to be strong, but not more fat."

Twenty-three years later, Juanita and her pastor/husband, Luis, were finally able to leave the country. Eventually, they arrived in Florida. What follows is her story, in her own words, of her survival in Fidel Castro's Cuba.

> In 1965, fifty-one pastors were put in prison. One of them was my brother. One day, six boys of the military service came to stay with me. What was the problem? Just that I had to share with

them the little food that the government let me buy once a month. With all my love, I cooked everything I found in my kitchen. There were seven plates on the table. In each plate I put seven pieces of fruit and bananas. In the center was a tureen with all my month's rice. But, early the next morning, Mercedes arrived at the door, carrying a bowl of soup.

One day, an officer came to me and asked me to present myself at his office the following week. What would they want and what would I answer? You would not think it is pleasant to be seated between three to four policemen. Some of the questions were: How many days a week did we gather at the church? Did we have outdoor activities? How many members? And so on. After two or three hours, I was told, "Well, you should know that all of your gatherings should be inside the church and never outside. If you do not obey, you will be taken to court". I agreed and asked if I could leave. An officer said, "Who told you you could leave?" as he hit his desk with his hand. I smiled and said, "Forgive me, I am not in a hurry to leave."

Another officer came to my home asking for information about the church. Do you know what I did? I told him that I was not going to give him any information regarding the members of the church because he had their addresses and could ask himself.

One day I went to God, knelt before him, and prayed, "Dear Lord, if it please you, if it does not offend you, I want to spend the rest of my missionary years with a servant of yours." On the same week of January, a servant of God, who was a widower, was praying and asking the Lord for a partner. We celebrated one of the most blessed weddings ever realized in my brother's church in the city of Regla!

When my new husband's son was released from prison, the government, by a miracle, allowed him to leave. He moved with his wife and three children to his sister's home in Venezuela. How difficult, how sad, how empty our hearts were when our son left.

There are unforgettable dates for every human being. For me, December 15, 1983, was one of those. About 11 P. M., in the Caracas, Venezuela, airport, we were receiving our suitcases. We looked toward the receiving area, and our heart jumped with joy. There were our children waiting for us. Even though we arrived in an unknown land, it meant that we were free. We were only able to bring a little suitcase for both of us and not one penny.

I was seven years old when I first saw an American person. I used to say, "If I were not Cuban, I would like to be 'Americana.'" That is why I am so happy to live in this country since July 11, 1987. Wonderful, cordial, and purveyor country! Now, instead of a small suitcase, we brought from Venezuela six of them. And I got my driving license.

Moving

While displacement was not so far away for Larry's family, they, too, sought to adjust to relocation. He realized a dream, but found that the detachment was slow.

It was a great opportunity. Years of work and graduate study had finally afforded me the opportunity I had longed for. It was something we had anticipated and planned for. It was something we wanted. It should have been easier. Saying goodbye had never been that difficult. After all, I'd grown up saying goodbye as my father accepted promotions. I'd always considered leaving to be a challenge—a new adventure to be faced

But here we were on Christmas Eve, in the church we loved so much, in the service that was our favorite one of the year. We were hanging on for dear life. There were lots of tears, and I don't know if we would have made it down the aisle for communion had it not been for friends who supported us as we walked toward the front.

As we left the church after the service, I came face-to-face with my friend and pastor. I will never forget the way I held on. I held on because I knew that when I let go, my heart would break.

It's been almost a year since we left, and we have not found an adequate replacement for our faith family. We've not found a church that touches us, that moves us to action, that holds us as close as that church did. Twice we've been back for visits, and each time we find ourselves doing well with everything but goodbyes. The pain of leaving is re-visited, and the hurt fills our hearts.

Certain factors make it easier for us to endure. Our family unit has been strengthened by the move. We've had no choice but to pull even closer together and depend on each other. With new friends, we are building an informal sort of family. We have made an earnest effort to keep in touch with our former faith family. A friend said, "What you hold in your heart is never very far away."

Though change for adults is difficult, the displacement of children is especially painful. They sometimes don't have the understanding to accept it. "Beth" had to console her own children. Then she discovered that her grandsons needed a new home. Her account of the events follows.

My husband was in the active military service and spent a great deal of time away from home. As the children grew older, it became more and more difficult for me to play the role of both parents.

The year that our son, Ted, was a junior in high school, we had to transfer to another state. He was very reluctant to make the move with us. It was the summer of 1973.

Both our son and daughter adapted rather well to the new area. Since our son was driving age, he was allowed more liberties. My husband was required to be away on flights overseas, sometimes staying away from home for weeks at a time. Without our knowledge, Ted had begun to have the wrong kind of friends. He got involved with drugs. He started skipping school and finally dropped out completely during the last few months of his senior year. This was a grave disappointment to us.

One evening, in May, 1975, when my husband and I came home from work, Ted and his girlfriend, Dianne, met us outside, stating that they had something to tell us. Their news was that Dianne was pregnant and that they wanted to get married. Ted was only 17 and a high school dropout. We unsuccessfully tried to talk them out of marriage. They were married in mid-June.

Ted realized he had to do something about his education to be able to support his family. He decided to sign up for a tour in the Air Force. He left the very day that his son, Jason, was born.

With the arrival of the baby, our lives were never the same. Unfortunately, Dianne was not a very good mother, primarily because of her age. She was a late sleeper, and she did not let the fact that she had an infant keep her from doing just that. Every day I came home from work for lunch, gave the baby a bath, fed him, and awakened Dianne. This went on for almost the entire time that Ted was away.

In the meantime, Dianne stayed on the go with her friends. Unknown to us, she had been seeing another man while Ted was gone. Their marriage was like a roller-coaster, constantly up and down. Ted and Dianne were both indulging in substance abuse, barely getting by financially and otherwise. In March, 1978, Debbie had another baby, whom they named Jacob. Shortly afterward, Debbie, Jason, and Jacob moved out of town to be near Debbie's mother.

The next year, Ted finished his four-year tour in the Air Force and was discharged. He decided that he would have a more stable life if he moved closer to us. He and the boys moved in with us. Dianne was to join them later. She decided that she did not want to come and that she wanted a divorce.

Ted drifted more and more into bad habits and further away from us. My husband and I were left with complete responsibility of the boys while our son worked during the day and played until all hours of the night.

Finally, we insisted he had to straighten up or get out. He chose to get a place of his own. We kept the children most of the time. He began drinking quite heavily. In March, 1981, Ted was arrested for suspected rape. All of the heartache and problems we had experienced since 1975 did not compare to this bombshell in our lives. We mortgaged our home to obtain a lawyer to represent him. The financial burden was almost more than we could endure.

Ted was found guilty and sentenced to 15 years in prison. When Dianne found out all that had happened, she came one night with her mother and took the boys. We had no legal papers to keep them. Even though our son had custody before he was put in jail, he certainly couldn't keep that privilege afterwards. After a period of time, she remarried and we were able to pick up the boys every other weekend.

In the summer of 1986, Ted developed a medical condition that caused him a lot of distress. It was discovered that he had a large malignant tumor on his adrenal gland that had encompassed a portion of his liver. Surgery was inevitable. He was scheduled for chemotherapy, but only slight, temporary improvement was seen. He died in December, 1986, 18 days after his 29th birthday. Needless to say, our lives have not been the same since.

Dianne gave us full custody of Jacob and Jason after our son's death. They have very little contact with their mother. She has been married four times since she divorced Ted and is currently divorced from her last husband.

For a long time, Dianne promised the boys that they would soon be coming to live with her. They finally realized she was giving them empty promises. Our lives now are devoted to getting Jason and Jacob educated and on the road to happy and successful lives of their own.

According to a report published in *U. S. News and World Report,* the problem of grandparents having to raise their grandchildren is extensive.

Three million children in the United States . . . live with their grandparents—an increase of almost 40 percent in the past decade . . . nothing can really ease the unique burdens these grandparents bear. Many of them are racked by shame and guilt at the fact that their own children have failed as parents—and many blame themselves, wondering where they went wrong as parents. In order to provide safe and loving homes for their grandchildren, some must emotionally abandon their own abusive or drug-addicted children. The stresses are compounded by the fact that some of the children they inherit are among the most needy, most emotionally damaged, and most angry in the nation.[3]

Nationally, more than 150 support groups exist for grandparents.[4]

Abandonment

Because of a variety of family problems, many children know separation from those they love. Millie was a very young child when she first knew abandonment from her own parents and, thus, displacement.

My early years were not a pretty picture. If described as a painting, the only colors on the canvas would be grey and black.

My parents were divorced when I was 16 months old. They gave me to an aunt to be raised. Daily, her children reminded me that I did not really belong to them. Consequently, I grew up feeling rejected. The greyness of not knowing why my parents gave me away, tinged with the blackness of feeling I must not be worth very much, colored my life. Much of my early life was spent in trying to gain acceptance by trying to please people. It was an attempt to fill a huge emotional void. This led to a rather drab and colorless existence. Looking back, I see that the pursuit of acceptance was really a quest for *self-acceptance.*

During my 20's and early 30's, feelings of rejection continued to shade my life. A person who has been rejected will ultimately reject himself and pass it on to others. My self-rejection manifested itself in a multitude of psychomatic symptoms and hostility toward those whom I loved the most.

We started attending a new church, and I soon found the perfect outlet for my feelings of rejection. Acceptance could be gained through performance! It wasn't long before I thought that what I *did* was what I *was.* Although this was a counterfeit solution to my problem, it did add color to my life. The colors were loud and splashy, like an abstract painting created by throwing a can of every color of paint there is onto a cheap canvas. During this time, my mother became ill and died. For me, it was the ultimate abandonment and rejection.

In my mind is painted a portrait of God's unconditional love. This reminds me that acceptance and identity are not based upon pleasing people, nor upon my performance. I cannot do one thing that will make God love me more. And, I cannot do one thing that will cause God to love me less! God just loves me the way I am. I am grateful that I discovered that. It is the only complete antidote to rejection.

Another account of abandonment follows Millie's story.

It was a Sunday morning in May, 1963. Around 9:15 A. M., a nurse in a doctor's clinic was tidying up the waiting room when she heard a tiny baby cry. The sound came from the direction of a sofa. What she saw in the corner of the sofa both shocked and amazed her. She found a baby girl, wrapped in a face towel with yellow daisies on it and a striped bath towel. Written on the inside half of a letter-size envelope and attached to the towel was the following note:

> HER NAME IS SUSAN ANNETTE & WAS
> BORN 5-11-63 AT 11:00 AM. PLEASE
> SEE THAT SHE IS TAKEN CARE OF
> SHE IS HUNGRY TOO. PLEASE DON'T
> CALL POLICE.

The nurse summoned a co-worker, and they immediately called the police. "Chief Dennis" and "Officer Mendoza" arrived at the clinic.

The baby appeared to be in good health. Her eyes had been cleaned and a liquid put into them. She had not been bathed, possibly just wiped clean. The area outside the building was searched, but the officers found no clue. One of the clinic doctors arrived. He did not know to whom the baby belonged, but he stated that as some of the patients were leaving and he was arriving, he noticed a 1962 Ford Galaxie convertible coming down the alley. Later, as he was leaving, he saw the car, driven by a woman, leave. He noticed the direction the car was going and later saw what he thought was the same car parked in front of a house.

The officers went to that house. "Tony Mendez" answered the door. The police questioned him and discovered that he had a 16-year-old wife. He showed the police his car, where they found dried blood. His wife explained that her husband had hit her on the nose. She did have a black eye. Inside the house, the officers found more blood on the floor of the living room, in another room, and on clothing. The couple agreed to come to the police station. They were interviewed further, and the wife consented to a medical exam. Doctors concluded that "Janice Mendez" could not possibly have recently given birth. She said that she had been to a hospital emergency room for treatment of her nose, but police failed to verify it. Police were suspicious that the couple had assisted in a birth.

The abandoned baby was taken to a local hospital where she was held until she was released to a social service agency. She was a beautiful baby, with a round face and a rosebud mouth. No other information was obtained in the case, and police were unable to complete the puzzle.

The next day, in another part of town, a young wife and mother of a three-year-old son was reading the local newspaper when she saw the headline "Mother Leaves Note with Baby." She said to her husband, "I hope we get this baby." The couple had already applied to adopt a baby girl. Within a few weeks, Susan was placed in that young couple's home. They named her Lisa, changed her birthdate by a few days so that she could not be traced, and eventually moved to another town.

Lisa grew up, a carefree, fun-loving girl. When she was 18, she married. When she found she was pregnant, she contacted the adoption agency to find what medical problems her child might inherit. Her adoptive parents had told her that she was adopted but not that she was abandoned. They had every intention of telling her later, but she discovered it by way of a letter from the adoption agency.

At the age of 28, Lisa decided to go back to the small town of her birth in an effort to find her birth mother. An article was placed in the newspaper stating the reason for her arrival. Within a few days, she received a letter. Among other things, it said:

> When I read the article in the newspaper and saw your picture, it was like someone had knocked the breath out of me. You see, I gave birth to you.
>
> You were the most beautiful thing I had ever seen. However, I had already made an irrevocable decision. I took you to the doctor's office wrapped in a towel, I think it had gold or yellow flowers on it. I was a very frightened, naive young girl. I felt there was no one I could confide in and nowhere to turn.
>
> Through all these years, you have never been far away from my thoughts. I prayed that your childhood would be happy and loving and that your parents would be thankful for your very special life. . . . I often wondered where you were. Please don't try to find who I am or where I am. It would create huge problems at this point in my life. Give me time to think and to decide what I should do.
>
> The letter began "Dear Lisa," but for all these years you have been and will always be "Susan Annette" to me.

Three months later, Lisa received another letter. It read, in part:

> One day I feel you want to know me and learn about your heritage, and the next day my feelings are exactly the opposite: you want to find me to let me know how much you despise me and tell me no real mother could have given away her own child. . . .
>
> Why would it be important for you to know me after all this time? Can I speak to you anonymously and not want to see you or touch you?
>
> Even though I asked you not to try to find me, I feel you need to have your questions answered and mine too.
>
> I'm thinking of you.

On the day after her birthday, Lisa received a phone call. The woman caller sounded middle-aged and well-educated but frightened. "I know you would like to know your medical background," she said. She knew of no one in the family with serious illnesses that could be inherited by Lisa's son. The call lasted three to four minutes. It ended when the caller began crying and said, "I have to go now."

Lisa hopes for more contact with her birth mother. But the communications are more than she had when she began her search. She will continue to seek. She knows now that she has two loving families. She has survived her own displacement.

Lisa is the author's own adopted daughter.
I wish you success, "Susan," in finding your "roots."

Notes

[1]Mark Luttrell, *Behind Prison Walls* (Nashville: Broadman Press, 1974) 55.
[2]Ibid., 69.
[3]16 December 1991, 80, 82.
[4]Ibid., 89.

Chapter 5

Weekend Dad

It is a fantasy to think that two people can commit themselves in a marriage ceremony, move in together, and resolve all conflicts with everlasting love. There will *not* be perfect harmony. Sometimes the conflict is relatively minor and humorous, as seen in "Grace's" story. Sometimes it is so severe and ongoing, that the marriage can't be saved, as evidenced by "James'" story.

The breakup that sometimes comes in a union is painful for everyone. The death of a marriage is forever life-changing. Johnny Carson quipped about his failed marriage and a divorce settlement that was especially devastating financially: "I resolve that, if I ever again get hit in the face with rice, it will be because I insulted a Chinese person."[1]

In every marriage, there is always an extended family to contend with. Trouble with that extended family often begins even before the wedding ceremony, as the following story demonstrates.

Southern belles know unwritten rules about proper wedding gifts. Such essentials as toasters, blenders, electric knives, and microwave ovens are proper for shower gifts. Correct wedding gifts are items like china, silver, cut-glass bowls, brass candlesticks, or something antique.

"I married someone from Cleveland," one Alabama belle remembers. "He had a perfectly lovely family, but they had no idea about southern ways. They kept sending wedding gifts like electric clocks, Tupperware items, and even a tool kit. My mother had a fit because, of course, we were going to display the gifts in the dining room. Mother had tables set up and draped in white fabric. Friends could then drop by and look at the gift display."

She says her mother carefully put all the toasters and clock radios underneath the draped skirts at the gift table. When the Cleveland relatives arrived for viewing the table, their gifts were pulled out and displayed. After the Ohio contingent left, the gifts went right back under the table.

"My mother had a reputation to uphold. . . . We couldn't have a
toaster oven sitting next to all my Francis I silver. That would have just
been too tacky."[2]

Then, there is the ceremony itself, which can sometimes get
completely out of hand. One writer describes the complications of
a southern wedding.

Just getting the bridesmaids to act as a unit is somewhat like training for
the Rockettes. Everything is done with precision. Southern bridesmaids
must wear their hair in the exact same style when walking down the
aisle, and they must have it done by the exact same hairdresser. The
same goes for their makeup, the color of their nails, the color of their
lipstick, and the color of their shoes, which they dye to match exactly
the color of their gowns.

Dying your shoes purple in Montgomery might turn out a different
shade than dyeing your shoes purple in Macon. All bridesmaids must
have their shoes dyed at the very same shoe shop. This is essential....

It is also important for the girl who cuts the bride's cake to wear the
exact same shade of eyeshadow as the girl who cuts the groom's cake.
If not, it could throw off the whole theme of the reception, and that
would be a most upsetting way for a bride and groom to leave for their
honeymoon.[3]

Often if peace and harmony last through the wedding ceremony, the celebration is barely over before the "perfect relationship"
begins to falter.

"Grace" writes,

We had been married only a few months. We were traveling
back to see our parents during the Christmas holidays. "What are
we having for lunch?," I asked. "Probably just a sandwich," said
my husband, Ben. We were students and poor as church mice. I
didn't want "just a sandwich," but I *did* want to be cooperative.

We entered the restaurant, and the waitress came to take our
order. She looked at me. "I'll have a ham sandwich," I said. Then
she looked at Ben. "I'll have pork chops, mashed potatoes, and
green peas," he said. I looked at my bridegroom in disbelief.
How could he do this to me? "That's the meanest man I ever
met," I thought, "and to think *I've* married him." I began to cry,
a fact noted by the waitress and everyone else in the restaurant.

I ate very little of the sandwich.

Not until we got back to the car did I discover I also could have had pork chops, mashed potatoes, and green peas for the same price as the ham sandwich—it was the day's special. "Why didn't you tell me?" I asked, the sobs beginning all over again. After a few minutes, I dried my tears, the conflict was resolved, and the marriage was saved.

Separation and Divorce

Unlike "Grace's" story, the conflict in "James'" marriage was severe and ongoing. Everything looked normal on the outside, but inside everything was chaos. He is now recovering in a new and stronger marriage.

My childhood carried more than its share of trauma. I certainly brought considerable emotional baggage into the marriage. So did she. From the start, the marriage was a roller-coaster ride of emotional highs and terribly destructive lows. Finally, the marriage disintegrated entirely.

The marriage had looked normal on the outside. Others had even approached us for advice because they envied what they thought we had. Little did they know. Our relationship rotted from within. The marriage was destructive. My life became horrible. We withered and died, little by little, day by day. We were just dying differently, each on our own timetable.

New beginnings have now been made. I have been in a new marriage for awhile. It is strong and life-giving.

"Kathleen" could not solve the problems in her marriage either. Her marital joy turned to sorrow. Painfully, she tells of difficult days and broken promises. She and her children are now finding family togetherness at last.

I loved the man. He was charming, a stranger to none, and an educated officer in the United States Navy who later became an attorney. He was kind, generous, and a great deal of fun. He liked kids, liked my parents and family—really a too-good-to-be-true person. That's the key. He *was* too good to be true.

The more successful he became in his law practice, the more he drank. The more he drank, the more he saw himself as the savior of all. He was a people-pleaser who never turned down *any* case, always acted as the life of every party, and had a joke for every occasion.

On the outside, all looked perfect—Mr. and Mrs. America with nice children, two cars, a barbecue pit and a dog. But the inside was full of children in tears, missed birthday celebrations, broken promises, verbal abuse, unbelievable language, late nights without coming in at all, wrecked cars, more anger, and more tension.

The trust I had cherished so much was gone. The commitment I had made I now realized was a one-way street ending in a dead end. I frantically searched for an answer. Because it angered him for me to read my Bible or to spend time praying, I slipped out of bed at 4:30 each morning and spent time with God, my coffee, and my dilemma. What could I do? Was I to wait until he was a statistic?

After many months, I finally mustered my courage. "You can kill yourself if you want to," I said, "but the kids and I are not going with you. Get help or leave." It must have been the strong words from a woman he was sure "had never had it so good." Surely he never expected her to defy the head of the household. At any rate, two days later, he checked into an alcoholic rehab unit on an outpatient basis.

The whole family went through treatment. In treatment, we met others whose problems were nearly identical. The behavior of an alcoholic is incredibly predictable. And spouses, like me, are predictably codependent.

Weeks passed, and the drinking stopped. The treatment and aftercare meetings continued. My husband lost his law practice and spent many hours doing nothing. He would tell us of going to support group meetings and expounding on how well he was doing. I was proud of him for not drinking, but the turmoil continued.

The tension in our house and the demolition of our spirits were growing. The longer he didn't drink, the more arrogant he became. I was tired—tired of fighting, tired of earning a living alone, tired of coming home to dissension and a house full of dirty dishes, dirty clothes, newspapers, coffee cups, and cigarette butts.

While I got a business up to full steam, the job of parenting and dealing with a man frozen in place, unable to get a job (was everything too menial?), was very nearly a load I could no longer manage. Two years after entering the alcoholic treatment center, his behavior was worse. True, he was not drinking. But, I was living with a dry-drunk who was convinced that the world had handed him a bum rap. He blamed me for the numerous affairs he'd had, the system for destroying his law practice, the secretary for not getting motions filed, and his colleagues for "whatever."

We talked. I prayed. We talked. We sought the help of psychologists and psychiatrists. The bottom line was: He had never reached his real bottom and would probably drink again. He was diagnosed as narcissistic, which came as no surprise. His entire existence centered around what was good for him.

Finally, I asked him to leave. He couldn't believe it. I hoped that making him leave a safe environment would help. To lose his family would certainly turn him around. He left, and *all* of us cried. It was the death of a dream.

He didn't turn around. At the end of two more years of separation, I proceeded to finalize the divorce. Laughter returned to our house, and freedom moved back in to take her place in the family. No longer did we have to *pretend* that everything was okay. We were now able to share feelings and to do chores together. From the oldest to the youngest, all three kids became responsible, hard-working, dedicated people.

Going through 23 years with a man I once loved, and still do in a very different way, has brought me to a new understanding of myself and my world. There are still struggles, moments of sheer panic, disappointments and tears. But, overall, I know we'll make it.

Like "Kathleen," "Sam" struggled with the death of a dream. He knew the pain of betrayal in a marriage. He survived and later found happiness in a second union.

Like many other couples, perhaps, we wanted to appear as if we were a happy family. We had many things going for us. But something was missing—we struggled. We felt that we were not getting what we needed spiritually. We finally decided to leave the church we were married in and search for a new church. We thought we were on our way, making progress.

We became involved with an organized group of couples in our new church. All of us seemed to be looking for ways to communicate with our marriage partners and to identify as well as express our feelings. As time went on, my wife and I found ourselves moving farther and farther apart, as were other couples in the group.

When discussions and opinions revealed who we really were, some members related better to other members of the group than to their own spouses. It became obvious that I was in that situation. My marriage was in jeopardy. I found notes my wife had written to another member of the group. I found secretive notes hidden away. I was one of nine people whose families were breaking up. I felt as if I had been destroyed.

At this point, there seemed to be nothing I could do. Divorce was evident. I had many questions. Why was this happening to me?

I felt support from my family in spite of their hurt. I began to wrap myself up in my job. Though I still felt betrayed, I didn't seek counseling or a support group. There are many more opportunities today for an individual in this situation to receive help than there were then.

After a year or so, I found myself dating. I was afraid, however, that the same thing could happen again. After several months passed, I realized I needed to stop feeling sorry for myself and get on with my life. The church really was supporting me with love. It was that kind of church.

For those who read this book, have faith. There may be some dark moments, but God is there.

Marriage was intended to eliminate loneliness as two join their lives together. How, then, can there be loneliness in a marriage? Many a couple has experienced it even while living together. Many have spoken of it, as C. W. Smith has shown in his collection of stories. The words below betray the loneliness.

Not only did I not know her. I felt unknown to her. I had complained that I wasn't close to Janice because I felt lonely. That people could be lonely in a marriage was new and disturbing to me. When I was jogging, I'd pass a pair of lovers lying nose-to-nose in the grass and I'd feel a surge of almost uncontrollable jealousy. I yearned to be in love.[4]

Loneliness and isolation are also difficult problems for divorced persons to overcome. After a marriage disintegrates, the feeling of being unneeded is almost overwhelming.

One father could scarcely accept his feelings of being unnecessary and unneeded.

> I left the living room window and went to stir the sauce. Would they miss my spaghetti? I went into Nicole's bedroom. I had painted the walls, the woodwork, the chest of drawers. I had put shelves in the closet. I was the only one tall enough to change the bulb in the overhead fixture. I could make her record player work when the switch on the lid was on the blink. I had given her a pride of stuffed animals that lined her bookshelves and lay in a herd asleep on her unmade bed. I would not be here to recite her goodnight poem—"Good night/Sleep tight/Wake up bright in the morning light/To do what's right with all your might"—or to read *Curious George* aloud. I would not be here to fix the flat on her bike, to watch her do a trick with her baton, or to fix Barbie's leg.
>
> The sadness of it weighed on me. I sat on the bed with my head in my hands. I cursed myself. At that moment, what I wished for most intensely was that I loved Janice and that Janice loved me as much as I wanted and needed to be loved. Then, none of this suffering would be necessary.[5]

As in the story above, in the course of the fragmentation of a marriage, many parents will assume their role only part-time. This requires a concentrated effort to survive and to find other things to fill the emptiness.

Part-time Parents

A "weekend dad" speaks of the camaraderie he feels to other part-time dads.

> When I took my kids to the zoo, I noticed other fathers without partners and instantly knew their story. We could distinguish each other from the regular, full-time dads merely giving mom a break because they were allowed to look bored. When I took them to a G-rated movie on Saturday afternoon, single parents would be the only adults in the audience—you could see their heads sticking up here and there down the rows like large cabbages in a rank of beets—and I'd think *there's*

another Uncle Dad trying to get through the day, because regular fathers just sent their kids there. In fast-food joints, I'd notice men sitting alone over cold pizzas and staring into space while their charges played video games.[6]

Losing a full-time child can cause a terrible grief, but among the greatest sufferers of divorce are the offspring of the failed union. It takes one or two years for children to cope with the acute stress of divorce and to begin recovery.

The parents must deal with:
•A break in finances
•The stress of finding new and adequate finances
•Role overload
•The pressure of finding and maintaining satisfying adult relationships.

All of this carries over to the children who must deal with:
•Lack of adult support as parents take on more responsibility
•Failure, social rejection, low self-esteem
•New parents and siblings (80% of divorced people will remarry).[7]

Telling the Children

Nothing equals the moment of telling the children about the breakup of the marriage, as one father relates. Then the children also must find a way to survive. Smith records this moment in the following account.

> "So, what do you think?" I finally asked.
> Keith shrugged, which I interpreted to mean indifferent or stoic acceptance. Now I know he felt helpless, numb, and utterly confused.
> "Just a separation," said Nicole.
> "Yes," I said, "just a separation." A legalistic truth: I was ninety-nine percent certain we would be divorced, but that remaining one percent permitted me the luxury of cowardice. "I'll see you all the time," I added. "I won't go away." This I truly wanted to believe.[8]

Sara, age 12, tells of that terrible day in her life.

Finally, when school ended, I was happy that the day was over but scared of what I might find at home. I tried to think of excuses for me to stay away from home for at least an hour or so. I decided to have a soda with a couple of friends. I called home to tell my Dad, and before he could say anything, I hung up! When people decided to leave, I decided to face what might be waiting for me at home.

The bus ride home seemed really quick. As I entered the building, just as yesterday, I got this strange feeling. As I headed toward my front door, I made sure to get out my keys and open the door myself. As I turned the key, my mother opened the door. This was a shock, since she was never home when I got home from school. The first thing she said was, "Your father has something to tell you." I walked very slowly. When I reached my father's working area, I looked at him. He seemed very sad and solemn.

I sat down. Neither of us talked. We just sat there in silence until my father started to say something. But then, he dropped it. He started soon again with, "As you might have noticed, the atmosphere around here has been slightly strained and uncomfortable lately."

I agreed, and then he went on. "Your mother and I have decided to separate!"

We were both silent. After a couple of minutes, I burst out in tears. I just cried, nothing else—didn't talk, didn't scream at Dad or Mom, didn't run out of the room. I just cried.

After I could control myself, I noticed that Dad was crying too! I went over and hugged him, not for much of a reason but just because I loved him.[9]

Like Sara, ten-year-old Jimmy also knew the heartbreak of his parents' divorce. His mother had moved to Florida.

Sometimes my mom phones me, and sometimes she writes me letters, but what I'd really like is the opportunity to see her and meet my two new half-sisters. Even though I've gotten used to living without her and I've mostly forgotten what she looks like, I do think about her all the time. For a while, I had a fantasy of running away to Florida, but that's pretty much died. . . . Still, it really hurts me that my own mother hasn't been able to see me. She's always writing that she'll come up, but she never makes it.

She tells me it would cost too much money and that she's too busy with her kids.[10]

One teenage girl wrote of the end of her parent's marriage and her survival of the ordeal.

> Dear Lord,
> it seems that sometimes my hardest trial stands when things in life don't exactly go according to my plans. Please help me, Lord, have patience when I cannot sing life's song.
> For if I walk beside you, You will not lead me wrong.
> Give me courage to continue.
> Give me faith to still believe.
> When everyone else has walked away,
> You said you'd never leave.
> Sometimes, Lord, I start crying
> Because I just don't understand.
> Help me wipe away my tears
> And then grab me by the hand.
> But most of all, Lord, help me remember
> That you have a perfect will
> And when on earth it seems there is no
> love
> That you will love me still.
>   "Kristine"

"Jan," age 21, expected her parents' divorce but still had trouble coping with it. With great courage, she tells of the changes in her family. It wasn't fair, but she was forced to say "goodbye." She has later found that some of the wounds are healing.

> I can't really remember a time in my childhood when my father wasn't drinking. He always had a beer or a drink of some other kind in his hand after work and all day on the weekends. Whether doing yard work or watching a football game, beer seemed a necessity for him to do anything.
> I don't think I knew my dad was an alcoholic until the Sunday we had a family meeting and Dad confessed, with tears in his eyes, that he had a problem. We all went into counseling at a treatment center. Though the beer went out of the refrigerator, nothing had changed.

My father is what is termed a "dry-drunk." I don't have a textbook explanation, but what it meant to my family was that Dad was no different than before he stopped drinking. Every quirk about his personality remained the same. He was hot-tempered and irrational. He was still a compulsive liar who sought only to please himself. Family was at the very bottom of his priority list, along with integrity and the unconditional love that should be natural between father and children.

I was in high school when my Dad moved out. After dark, we loaded part of our living room furniture and my sister's twin bed into the station wagon for him. I can't say for sure, but I think at that time there was still hope for us to be a whole family.

Dad moved from place to place without telling us when or where he was moving. It seemed he moved in with one girlfriend after another. . . . It didn't surprise us that girlfriend after girlfriend kicked him out.

I went to college in the fall of 1989. In December of that year, my parents' divorce was finalized. It wasn't that I didn't think it would happen, I just don't think you can ever be fully prepared for a separation from your security.

Forgiveness for me was not an overnight thing. It still takes a conscious effort every day for me to put behind me all the cruel things my father said and did and for me to *truly* forgive. He lives in another state now. He moved there in October, 1990, without telling any of his three children. Had we not searched for him, I am sure we never would have heard from him again. He is still running from the reality of his past. Some days it is easier for me to forgive than others. He still says and does hurtful things.

God knows my every need before I know how to ask. He provides faithfully every day . . . but it hasn't been easy. God isn't there to hold me when I hurt. He isn't the best father to play football with, and He isn't downstairs to light the fire on Christmas morning.

Sometimes it takes hard work, tears, and sweat to make it day to day. But, it's worth it. The wounds are healing; the tears are being wiped away.

Parents of Divorced Persons

"Jan" knows the terrible tearing-away of a day-to-day father/child relationship and how difficult it is to recover from the loss.

In addition to spouses and suffering children, there are also the forgotten persons in a divorce—those who try to hide their tears so no one knows. Included in those are the sometimes grieving parents of a recently divorced son or daughter, who must adjust to the changes. The mother of a daughter, recently divorced, writes:

> He came into our lives with kindness—this man who chose our daughter to be his wife. That's the thing we won't forget about him, his gentleness to us and to her. We felt good about the marriage, as if he were the one planned just for her all along.
>
> It was shattering, then, to find that the marriage hadn't worked. Something had gone wrong. My husband and I didn't feel we were to blame. We felt that we had drawn him into our circle of family and made him a part of it. We had looked forward to years of enjoying him, this special person.
>
> There would be no more family dinners when we laughed with him. Perhaps that was hardest of all—seeing that empty chair at all family celebrations—a place that no one could fill the way he did. There would be no more photographs of family times that included him.
>
> But, we had to accept the termination of the marriage. We couldn't put the broken pieces back together. With the passage of years, we would forget somewhat, but it was like a death. Things would never be the same because he was gone. It was like losing a son.
>
> Nevertheless, we are recovering from the blow and perhaps someday we'll accept another young man into our lives. Maybe we'll feel, too, that he's the right person for that time. After all, a part of being a parent is wanting to see our children happy in fulfilling relationships. Time heals. At least, we're counting on it.

With the help of friends, family, and support groups, many people are finding that one can survive the death of a marriage and build a new life that is rewarding.

Notes

[1]James A. Albert, *Pay Dirt: Divorces of the Rich and Famous* (Boston: Brandon Publishing Co., 1989) 261.

[2]Marilyn Schwartz, *A Southern Belle Primer, Or Why Princess Margaret Will Never Be a Kappa Kappa Gamma* (New York: Doubleday, 1991) 77.

[3]Ibid., 73.

[4]C. W. Smith, *Will They Love Me When I Leave?* (New York: Putnam Publishing Group, 1987) 85.

[5]Ibid., 97.

[6]Ibid., 111.

[7]From a lecture by Sue Fisher, Kirkwood High School, 23 February 1989.

[8]C. W. Smith, 101.

[9]Jill Krementz, *How It Feels When Parents Divorce* (New York: Alfred A. Knopf, 1984) 39.

[10]Ibid., 34.

Chapter 6

Can Love Let Go?

I looked in the box. "It's the stuff I *don't* want to take to college," he had said. It was amazing. I found a sweaty cap that hadn't been washed all summer and tennis shoes that Goodwill wouldn't want. There was also a concert ticket stub (from the one I prayed he wouldn't be trampled to death at), letters and photos from broken romances, and multiple screws that fit Heaven knows what. There were overdrawn bank drafts, an electrical "something" I couldn't recognize, and his Christmas cards that never got mailed.

How could anyone go off for four years and leave a room in this condition? *Four years* or, perhaps, forever. As I sat among the rubble, the tears came. I could not stop them.

Leaving the Nest

Others also agree that saying "goodbye" to a much-loved son or daughter is crushing. Cal Thomas, writer of a syndicated column, speaks his feelings in sending his last child off to college:

It's the silence you notice first when the last child has left home for college. The ceiling fans still whir, the telephone and doorbell still ring; the wooden floors occasionally creak and the cat meows. But the difference is that these sounds now seem hollow and disconnected.

Perhaps it is not silence, but the absence of noise that is noticed: The loud music no longer comes through the locked bedroom door; feet as large as shoe boxes no longer bound up and down stairs, doors are not slammed. These sounds were evidence of another person in the house who helped to make it a home.

I had told friends I would never suffer from "empty nest syndrome." Not me. That was for the sentimental and those who had no interests outside of family. I was looking forward to the freedom a house empty of children would bring; to travel at a moment's notice, to go out to dinner without consulting a child's schedule, to leave the bedroom door open.

He has been gone only 24 hours, and already I miss him. I miss the joy I feel when I see him, the identification that comes from knowing we belong to each other. I talked to him on the phone last night less than seven hours after saying goodbye. I still miss him.[1]

The process of detachment, separation, and saying goodbye to those we love is a painful event in our lives. Often great pain accompanies *involuntary* detachment—a child goes to college or moves away, a husband goes on a long business trip, we are forced to move away from our family of origin, or we have no communication with an elderly relative because of his mental state. Separations are inevitable in our lives. We must pick ourselves up and go on. As the stories in this chapter will attest, it's possible to survive painful separations.

One of the best narratives ever written on separation and detachment comes from James Dobson's book *Hide and Seek*. Dobson wrote a suggested letter for a mother to send to her 20-year-old son at a time when it was necessary for her to let go of him. It is printed here for your reflection.

Dear Paul:

This is the most important letter that I have ever written to you, and I hope you will take it as seriously as it is intended. I have given a great amount of thought and prayer to this matter I want to convey, and I believe I am right in what I've decided to do.

For the past several years, you and I have been involved in a painful tug-of-war. You have been struggling to free yourself of my values and my wishes for your life. At the same time, I have been trying to hold you to what we both know is right. Even at the risk of nagging, I have been saying, "Go to church," "Choose the right friends," "Make good grades in school," "Live a Christian life," "Prepare wisely for your future," etc. I'm sure you've gotten tired of this urging and warning, but I have only wanted the best for you. This is the only way I knew to keep you from making some of the mistakes so many of the others have made.

However, I've thought it all over during this last month, and I believe that my job as your mother is now finished. Since the day you were born, I have done my best to do what was right for you. I have not always been successful—I've made mistakes, and I've failed in many ways. Someday you will learn how difficult it is to be a good parent, and perhaps then you'll understand me better than you do now. But there's one area where I've never waivered: I've loved you with everything that is within me. It is impossible to convey the depth of my love for you through these years, and the affection is as great today as it has ever been. It will continue to be there in the future, although our relationship will change from this moment. As of now, you are free! You may reject God or accept Him, as you choose. Ultimately, you will answer only to Him anyway. You may marry whomever you wish without protest from me. You may go to U.C.L.A. or U.S.C. or any other college of your selection. You may fail or succeed in each of life's responsibilities. The umbilical cord is now broken.

I am not saying these things out of bitterness or anger. I still care what happens to you and am concerned for your welfare. I will pray for you daily, and, if you come to me for advice, I'll offer my opinion. *But the responsibility now shifts from my shoulders to yours.* You are a man now, and you're entitled to make your own decisions—regardless of the consequences. Throughout your life, I've tried to build a foundation of values which would prepare you for this moment of manhood and independence. That time has come, and my record is in the books.

I have confidence in you, son. You are gifted and have been blessed in so many ways. I believe God will lead you and guide your footsteps, and I am optimistic about the future. Regardless of the outcome, I will always have a special tenderness in my heart for my beloved son.

Sincerely,
Your mother[2]

The Pain of Detaching

The pain of the mother in the foregoing letter is evident. Often we find it necessary to detach forcefully from someone we love for a variety of reasons. Now we are speaking of a *voluntary* "letting go" (though unwillingly in our hearts we are saying "No, I don't want this.") We could also call it a separation with a fixed purpose. It is not a cold, antagonistic withdrawal. It is not so much aloofness and selfishness as *self-preservation*. It does *not* include picking up the pieces of the broken lives caused by the mistakes of the people we love.

In her book, *Codependent No More*, Melanie Beattie says,

I hope you will be able to detach with love for the person or persons you are detaching from. I think it is better to do everything in an attitude of love. However, for a variety of reasons, we can't always do that. If you can't detach in love, it is my opinion that it is better to detach in anger rather than to stay attached. If we are detached, we are in a better position to work on (or through) our resentful emotions. If we're attached, we probably won't do anything other than stay upset.

When should we detach? When we can't stop thinking, talking about, or worrying about someone or something; when our emotions are churning and boiling; when we feel like we *have* to do something about someone because we can't stand it another minute; when we're hanging on by a thread and it feels like that single thread is frayed; and when we believe we can no longer live with the problem we've been trying to live with. It is time to detach![3]

A good example of the need to detach comes from a parent who said:

We have been suckers and patsies many different times, supplying funds for rent or a coat or some other necessity, not realizing that the money really goes to sustain a lifestyle of which we don't approve, friends who don't work, or a drug dependency. We have been hooked, manipulated, and conned by our children.[4]

Many people, like "Libby," discover that voluntary estrangement from a close family member is especially painful. She has demonstrated her ability to survive and recover.

I never could understand how a person could detach himself from a loved one until I was forced to do it for the sake of my survival. For me, it was done in gradual stages determined by the person and circumstances.

In my family, I am not certain who detached first. When I became aware of my son's serious drinking problems, he was 16 years old and in tenth grade. The school called me at work to tell me my son "Jeff" had ten unexcused absences, which would cause him not to pass the quarter. I was shocked. I would drop him off at school (front door, mind you!) and go on to the school where I taught. As a result of his absences, Jeff quit school. That really put the detachment process in motion. For the first time, I was made aware that I could no longer monitor his actions. As I had been a single parent for nine years, I had to work.

Following this event, it was understood that "Jeff" would secure a job and find out what it was like to live in the "real world." It was not a problem for him to get a job—keeping one was another story, as is the case with many alcoholics. That was the destructive path he was on.

With his new-found freedom, "Jeff" became involved with law problems, forcing me to get legal counsel when he was 17. He was not living at home (by his choice). I wanted to know what I was legally responsible for because of his many varied episodes. He had a car, in which he had several minor accidents and seventeen traffic violations—unpaid.

This accumulation of incidents made me very fearful. While at work one day, the local police called, indicating my son's car was parked illegally. They wanted to know what I wanted to do about it. After consulting with my attorney, I went with a friend to the police station. We had the car towed to a garage to be demolished. My fear was that my son would harm someone with his vehicle since the vehicle was in my name. You can imagine "Jeff's" reaction when he called to ask me if I knew where his car was. To say he didn't handle it well is an understatement.

I didn't hear from him or know where he was for several months. This became a behavior pattern to which I never adjusted. Every boy I saw with a letter jacket on who was about the size and approximate age of my son caused my heart to skip a beat. I thought it was him.

I realized I needed help. I called and found out about many programs for teenage alcoholics and what I could do. I heard about *Toughlove*. But, that wasn't what I wanted to hear. As I read the *Toughlove* book (see note 4), I tried to become more knowledgeable. As circumstances in our relationship became more intolerable, I realized being very tough was the way for me to go. Nothing I had said or done had worked. This was another step in the detachment process.

"Jeff" came back home to live, but he soon ended up in jail for drunk and disorderly conduct. Previously, there had been many other circumstances of inebriation. I was called to the police precinct to see him. My son wanted me to pay the money to bail him out. I refused. Drunk as he was, he understood what that meant—three days in jail. After much soul-searching, I was convinced that this was the lesson he needed. WRONG! As soon as he was released, which was sooner than the police told me, he came home, showered, changed clothes, and left to become inebriated again.

When he returned, I was waiting to meet him. Very calmly, I told him that he could no longer live at home, explaining that there was nothing further that I could do to help him. "I'll take you anywhere you want to go," I said, "but you can't stay in this home." "Jeff" called his father, and his father came to get him the next morning. When "Jeff" departed, I was so remorseful. I finally knew what it meant to detach with Toughlove.

That was eleven years ago. He has married and divorced since then. He has moved out of state. On two occasions, he has asked to come home. I have remained firm about him not returning home to live permanently.

I hope in the fullness of time, and with his eventual help and recovery, Jeff and I can have a fruitful, enjoyable, and enduring relationship.

Like so many other parents, "Libby" discovered that a parent may have to detach when a child becomes addicted. You can't live with him. You cannot make him recover from his addiction. He must do that himself.

Toughlove

"Disjoining" is especially difficult in the parent-child relationship. It's a parent's job to be protective, guiding, and to try to help mold a child's life for the best. It is especially painful, then, for a parent to watch a child head for disaster, back off, and allow that to happen.

The authors of *Toughlove* point out:

> Once in crisis, parents cling to their memories of those wonderful childhood years of togetherness and good feeling. Thinking that they can achieve that togetherness again, they appease their teenagers and have as much success as Chamberlain had with Hitler.[5]

The real danger in not letting go when necessary is that all of our bitterness, resentment, fear, hostility and hurt will affect the other relationships in our lives.

Just as painful as parents having to detach from a child, is having a child detach from parents for no obvious reason. "Rose" writes an especially poignant account of her daughter's detachment and of some positive reconciliation for both of them.

Our sons were two, three, and four years of age. We wanted a daughter to grow up with the boys. We adopted a beautiful baby girl. We all loved her dearly. Our sons were born *to* us and "Lynn" was born *for* us.

When our daughter reached her teen years, communication began to break down between us. Her personality changed from a sweet disposition to that of a stranger. She snapped hateful replies to our simple questions. She spent more and more time shut up in her room. We took her for counseling, but she would not cooperate.

I was an elementary teacher. I took advantage of the opportunity to get advice from the school counselor. I explained "Lynn's" flaring temper and my anger in response—the snowballing effect that followed. She said, "When you see this is going to happen, do one of three things: ignore what is said, come back with an absurd remark, or agree with her." It worked!

When Lynn graduated from high school, she went to Vermont. Unable to find work, she came back home. She got a job, and, for the first time, she really appreciated home. Except for one semester at a college, she worked and lived at home for seven years. We got along very well. We did not, however, enjoy the open sharing that all mothers would want with their daughters.

Then "Lynn" decided to attend another college. We paid all her school expenses. She got a part time job to finance her car and other personal expenses. Life seemed good for a year or so. We got mail regularly. Then, she was asked to work full time or give up her job. She chose the full time job. A few weeks later, there was a cutback, and she lost her job. Her world fell apart. She broke off communication with us. She was physically and emotionally ill.

I wrestled with my feelings of anger, sympathy, helplessness, love, hate, guilt, pity, and frustration. It was like holding the reins of a runaway horse. I spent many restless nights.

I expressed my thoughts in the following way:
Why does my heart ache so?
Why do I continue to hope
And long for you?
The hand outstretched in love—
    Rejected
    Crushed
    Extended once again.

Because of love—no other could explain
The hurt, the grief, the restlessness
Yet reaching out again
Was there no love, there could be no rejection
Can love let go? Can it be erased?
Is that a choice?
Could love forget?
No! Never!
Yet, if it were so
My heart would choose to love
With hand extended once again.

"Rose" tried letters, an example of which follows:

It has been almost eight months since you have talked or written to us. The only communications we had with you for two months before that were almost as hard as the silence. When you sent back your Christmas check uncashed with no comment, it was just another hurt among the many. If you only could have heard the excitement in your dad's voice when he saw a letter from you!

I can honestly say neither of us has the answer to why we are being rejected. So I tell myself "'Lynn' is sick."

I think about the fact that if I didn't love you, it wouldn't hurt. As I was thinking about that, I realized the more we love, the greater the hurt in being rejected.

Her parents received the following note from "Lynn":

Our phone conversations are uncomfortable and unpleasant for me. I can see no point in continuing that. I no longer want to be a part of it. There is nothing to discuss. There is nothing to explain. I don't want you to call me anymore. I don't want *any* form of personal contact. I have nothing further to say about any of this. I have nothing to say to anyone.

"Lynn"

Almost a year later, "Lynn's" life began to change, according to "Rose":

"Lynn" was told, if she didn't get help, she didn't have more than a year to live. She entered the eating disorders section of a hospital. We learned from someone where she worked that she was there. We wanted to visit her, or at least send a card. We were told there was no one in the hospital by that name. Prior to that time, she had changed her name legally (she told us about it years later, just before changing it back to our name.)

After "Lynn" was released, she began seeing some friends. After some time, she came to see us. Working back into the family has been a slow process for her. We learned from her that she had been involved in drug and alcohol abuse since those teen years. Her body suffers from that abuse as well as from anorexia and depression. I am thankful for a good relationship with her now. She has received her bachelor's degree in social work.

To "let go" does not mean to stop caring for the person you love or to cut yourself off completely from him. It does mean that, from this point on, you will not try to control his life or to prevent the consequences that inevitably come when he makes mistakes. He will now have to face reality on his own. The outcome is no longer in the hands of the "keeper."

To "let go" *does* mean that you admit powerlessness to help him. You cannot "fix" him or change his feelings toward you. No matter how much you want it, *you can't make him love you.* It often brings terrible loneliness—possibly the most crippling of all human emotions. On the other hand, letting go can sometimes mean great relief—as you realize, "I am no longer responsible for this person's debts, thoughts, feelings, obligations; I am free."

Release and Recovery

"Natalie" faced a painful disjunction for a different reason. It was necessary for her to call upon all of her resources when detaching from her husband. With much emotion, she tells of her survival and present recovery. It was unthinkable that events could have progressed as they did.

When I married in the 1950s, I expected it to be a lifetime commitment, as did my husband. I never dreamed I would need to detach from my spouse or have thoughts of divorcing him.

I had more than a nagging thought that my hubby was being unfaithful to me. We had been transferred back to the city that housed a divorcee with whom my spouse was involved in the past. There were signs: staying late in the office, choosing not to kiss me anymore, neglecting to tell me he loved me even when I said: "I love you" first, and those annoying "hang up" phone calls and secretive conversations that made me realize I could not trust him. Whenever I tried to talk to him about it, he either denied it or put me down.

I decided to go out of town. Before I left, however, I prayed for God to lead me, and especially to let me know if my spouse was unfaithful. When I arrived back home, one of our children telephoned to tell me that she had seen her dad in a public place holding hands with another woman. She even encouraged me to leave her father, whom she adored.

Now I had to take action. I felt terribly hurt. About eight months earlier, I had received similar information and was in the process of leaving my husband. That time he arrived home and talked me out of leaving. This time I didn't wait to be talked out of it by his charming personality. I quickly found suitcases and threw clothes, medicine, and toiletries into them. Jumping into my parked car, I left for a relative's house in a nearby town. On my way out of town, I passed my husband's car with the other woman sitting beside him. It was a confirmation to me that I had made the right decision.

When he contacted me, I requested he get into professional counseling so we could work on our marriage. After living within a loving family circle for two months, I realized I needed to make another decision. I needed to be on my own. It would be painfully lonesome, but living within an unloving relationship, I reasoned, is also painful, lonesome and demoralizing to one's character. Hanging on to him was poisonous to me. My self-esteem was at a low ebb. I really had nothing to lose and, perhaps, something to be gained by "letting go" of a broken relationship.

I do not regret acting on the wisdom of a separation. I went to my son's pastor for counseling. The pastor told me of support group meetings where people like me could meet and voice their codependency. I went to several meetings and learned of others' experiences. I told myself I had a right to be angry. My needs were not met, and I had been deceived and manipulated.

With great coincidence (or miracle), I stumbled upon an opportunity to get into a weekly class on "troubled marriages."

When I told my spouse about it, he wanted to go also! Both of us drove to the meetings in another town. I began by forgiving my spouse and not blaming him entirely for our troubles. i took steps to salvage the good parts of our marriage. I began to work on the present instead of the past.

I learned my strengths and weaknesses, too. My biggest offense to my husband was in "mothering him" him. I was unaware that I was doing it. I still bite my tongue many times to stop from hinting or suggesting things to him.

There were subtle changes in my husband, too. When we talked at lunchtimes, I sensed a greater respect, a growing concern, and more love for me. Jacob M. Braude wrote, "Consider how hard it is to change yourself, and you'll understand what little chance you have of trying to change others." Changing our own behavior patterns took time. I stepped out on faith and moved back to my husband.

"Goodbye" is a painful word. But, it doesn't have to be the end of the world for us. Through the support of others who have found it necessary to detach, we may find new relationships, while slowly letting go of the old ones.

Take this test.

1. Do you feel someone else is attempting to control you in ways that are unhealthy?

2. Do the wants and needs of others always come before your own needs?

3. Do you set aside very little time for your own needs?

4. Do you feel that you could never be playful, carefree, or trifling?

5. Have you lost your own interests, goals, and association with others?

6. Do you often feel that your existence is not really enjoyable and that you are merely a servant?

7. Do you take physical or emotional abuse and tell yourself "This too will pass"? (It seldom does!)

8. Do you feel good about yourself only if you have the approval of the person(s) you love?

If you answered "Yes" to most of the above, perhaps it is time to detach. It may only be with the help of others in similar circumstances that you will have the strength to do it.

Notes

[1]Cal Thomas, "Silence Is Golden? Don't Be So Sure," *Los Angeles Times Syndicate*, 1990. Reprinted by permission.

[2]James Dobson, *Hide or Seek* (Grand rapids: Fleming H. Revell Co., 1974) 101.

[3]Melody Beattie, *Codependent No More* (Center City, MN: Hazeldon Foundation, 1987) 58. Reprinted by permission.

[4]Phyliss York, David York, and Ted Wachtel, *Toughlove* (New York: Doubleday, 1982) 142.

[5]Ibid., 104.

Chapter 7

One Day at a Time

WOMAN IN THE BALCONY: Is there much drinking in Grover's Corners?

MR. WEBB: Well, ma'am. I wouldn't know what you'd call *much*. Sattidy nights the farmhands meet down in Ellery Greenough's stable and holler some. Fourth of July I've been known to taste a drop myself—and Decoration Day, of course. We've got one or two town drunks, but they're always having remorses every time an evangelist comes to town.[1]

When Thornton Wilder wrote those lines into his famous play *Our Town*, it was several years after the repeal of Prohibition in 1933. Stanton Peele has described the conditions of alcohol use at that time.

At that time, most Americans thought about alcoholism as Thornton Wilder did; it was a rare occurrence, something found among a few social pariahs. In addition, some lower types (like the farmhands down in Ellery Greenough's stable) were likely to get drunk on weekends and create quite a commotion. Most upstanding townspeople, like Mr. Webb, might be occasional drinkers, but they wouldn't make a regular habit of it.[2]

Alcoholism and Recovery

But today, alcoholism affects millions of Americans. One in three American families is now in need of recovery because of the disease. Many famous Americans have "owned up" to their problem—notably Doc Severinson, Billy Carter, Elizabeth Taylor, Betty Ford, Carrie Fisher and Drew Barrymore, among others. And it has become quite fashionable to go into treatment. Alcoholics learn that it is a lifelong disease that one can revert to at any time after treatment. So, an alcoholic must take recovery "one day at a time."

Drunkenness generally continues at a high level among adolescents and young adults in America. Ghetto and minority communities—particularly such minorities as Native Americans, Eskimos, Hispanics, and Blacks—have a high incidence of alcoholism.[3] The mortality rate from alcohol abuse for 15–24 year-old Native Americans in New Mexico is exceedingly higher than the Anglo rate. The problem is also growing among Caucasians.

Even the most "hopeless" of victims can recover. Robert Sundance's story proves that even someone who is "on the lowest rung of society's totem pole" can change "the system."

> Drunk, homeless, and living on skid row for more than 20 years, 200 times with the D.T.'s, arrested 500 times, and denied his legal rights, Sundance was determined to be heard in court. Over a ten-year period, he spent an average of 226 days in jail each year, waiting to plead his case. He believed that his jailings for public drunkenness were cruel and unconstitutional because his alcoholism was a disease.
>
> His life could have ended many ways. Alcohol could have killed him, as it did his drinking friends who died from cirrhosis of the liver before the age of 30. He might have had a heart attack from the D. T.'s while left unattended in the drunk tank, like others he knew who were cremated under false names. The elements could have finished him off while he slept in skid-row parking lots, blanketed by nothing more than the cheap wine in his body.
>
> Robert Sundance lived to fight and win. His landmark court case drastically reformed the process of arrest and treatment of public inebriates. In Los Angeles County, where the *Sundance Decision* was won, these arrests dropped from more than 50,000 to about 1,000 per year. He beat alcohol, has been sober for 12 years, and is executive director of the Indian Alcohol Commission of California.[4]

Included in the dangers of alcohol are drinking and driving, a combination that claims the lives of many. The drunk driver may spend years paying for his mistakes, as "Clarence" found out before his recovery began.

> In high school I was active in cross country and wrestling. I was on the honor roll my freshman year. At the end of my freshman year, I was introduced to alcohol. I began to skip classes, and

eventually I quit school. At the age of 17, I went back to school and quit again. One night, I went to a party 50 miles from home and found myself stranded. While under the influence of alcohol, I stole a truck in order to get home before the curfew my parents had set for me. A few days later, I was arrested and charged with auto theft. I was granted five years probation.

At 18, my parents told me to leave home. So, I absconded from probation and lived on the streets, traveling all over the United States. This venture lasted almost nine months. Then, I returned to my home town.

In November, 1982, I was hired by an outdoor advertising company. I really enjoyed my job. During this time, I sought and accomplished my Grade Equivalency Diploma. Three years later I was laid off. I decided to turn myself in to authorities for the long-overdue probation violation. The judge re-instated my probation with only three months to complete it.

In December, 1985, I was hired by another outdoor advertising company. Around Christmas time, with permission, I drove the company truck (with my best friend, Leon, as a passenger) home from my sister's wedding. I had tried to get Leon to leave the reception, but I let him talk me into staying. I had been drinking. I knew the risks of drinking and driving. I had an accident and rolled the truck. I knew that Leon was badly hurt. I held his hand, screaming at him, "Just hold on!" He gripped my hand and then started shaking. Then he bit down on his tongue and let loose of my hand. I screamed, "No!" But, I knew he was dead.

I went to Leon's parents' house. I had to tell them just what happened. It was the hardest thing I have ever done in my whole life. After talking to them, Leon's dad came up to me with a Christmas gift that Leon had bought me. My heart pounded. I cried. It was all I could do. A few days later I opened it. I knew I would never again be standing next to Leon, joking, kidding around like we used to. I couldn't bring him back. I can still hear his voice and laughter to this very day. We were best friends.

I was charged with a DWI and Involuntary Manslaughter and given three year's probation. I had violated the auto theft probation, however, and a conviction was then imposed. I denied being responsible for the accident. I looked at it only as an accident. I was also harassed by society and called a "killer."

In May, 1987, I had a terrific job lined up working for a sign company. I didn't find out about the effects of alcohol until I had one more accident. Two days before I was to start work, while under the influence of alcohol, I rear-ended a car and hurt someone. After the last accident, I learned how alcohol slows down the body reflexes. It puts the brain to sleep slowly after each drink. If someone had only told me about the dangers while I was in school, possibly this could have been avoided! I stopped drinking, then, and started attending self-help groups.

I was sentenced to a total of eight years in prison for Involuntary Manslaughter, DWI, second degree assault, and leaving the scene of an accident. Alcohol had almost completely destroyed my life. In prison, I attended church and support groups, planned workshops on alcohol awareness, and received my Associate of Arts degree in general education. I became involved in an Alcoholics Victorious support group. And, I found God.

I was released from prison to house arrest in December, 1990, and released from house arrest to parole in April, 1991. I am now working regularly, attending support group meetings, private counseling, and lectures. I could not have done it without the meetings and working the 12-steps of Alcoholics Anonymous in my everyday life.

Other Chemical Dependencies

The user of other drugs also finds recovery slow and painful.

Charlie McMordie was such a heavy drug user that eventually suicide seemed like his only escape. He drank heavily, used marijuana, LSD, speed, and other drugs. It was cocaine, however, that led to his downfall. He shot, snorted, and smoked cocaine until it cost him his marriage, job, family, friends, and fortune. Although family oil and cattle brought him more than $12,000 per month for some time, most of that money was spent on drugs.

For the 15 years he was addicted, McMordie did not think he had a drug problem. The grand mal seizures, ruined relationships, and constant use were second nature to him. His entire life centered around cocaine. He reluctantly entered treatment as a result of a family intervention, though he continued to deny having a drug problem until an incredible event ended his resistance.

Charlie no longer drinks or uses any drugs. He believes that so much as a single puff of marijuana could lead him back to cocaine and certain death. He now works as a counselor with chemically-dependent individuals and finds true happiness and meaning helping others who are struggling in their own recoveries.[5]

Addicted persons are truly captives in the sense that they are prisoners to their addictions. Oftentimes the addiction begins very early.

A teenager describes the change in his lifestyle.

I didn't start in heavy on drugs—an occasional joint with friends at a football game or party, that was it. But even that little bit led to alcohol and other drugs. I thought I could stop taking drugs. I started telling myself, "I can stop, I can stop." It didn't work. Then I told myself I was just having fun, that I could stop whenever I wanted to get serious. That didn't work either.

I started to lie to myself in other ways. I talked myself into believing that I was losing weight because I didn't like to eat. I refused to admit to myself that it was because all I wanted to put into my mouth were pills and alcohol. I lied to myself so much that, after a while, I couldn't tell the difference between the truth and a lie. Often I was in such a drugged fog that I didn't know what I was doing or where I was.

The more I used drugs, the more depressed I became. So I'd dope myself up even more in order to get a high. It got to the point where I couldn't bear life if I wasn't high.

My addiction forced my parents to pull me out of school. It really hurt my family. When one person in a family gets sick, it affects the whole family. Everybody gets out of balance.

I ignored anyone who told me I had a drug problem until my family and friends confronted me with facts about myself. Later, I found that they actually had planned and rehearsed the confrontation. They waited for a day when I was sober and took me by surprise. It was a shock that woke me up to a lot of things.

Eventually I was placed in a treatment center against my will. I made up my mind that I'd go through treatment by lying to everyone and telling them that I had straightened out so they'd get off my back. I figured I'd get out, then go back on drugs.

When I was in treatment, I had to come to terms with myself. It wasn't easy, especially when I woke up to the fact that I had depended on alcohol and drugs to deal with everything that happened to me during a routine day.

It's complicated to explain what treatment is all about. It's like coming down to earth with a hard bang. It's dealing honestly with your parents and others. It's dealing honestly with yourself. It's a matter of realizing what your feelings are, why you feel the way you do, and how to handle those feelings.

I stayed sober for about six months after I left treatment. Than I began to slip. I decided that, since I popped pills and smoked pot more than I drank, it was the pills and pot, not the alcohol, that wrecked me. I figured that I could drink again and keep it under control. Within two weeks, I was back in the same rotten shape I was a year before. I couldn't stop. That was the worst feeling—a feeling of failure because I wasn't using what I'd learned in treatment about how to stay sober. I bounded from high to low to low to high.

At the end of my two-week binge, I got involved with a local church group that helps troubled kids. The group did a lot to bring me around.

Now I can look back and see the grief and pain I felt and caused my family and friends. I realize that my family and friends saved my life.[6]

Eating Disorders

Besides those who are recovering from drug addictions, there are others who are recovering from problems caused by eating disorders. These maladies claim the lives of hundreds of persons. They disrupt families, school and job performance, and affect self-worth. The problems touch not only the victims but many others, including families and friends, who are unable to cope with it. The malady affects more women than men.

Characteristic of eating-disorder sufferers are: perfectionism, inability to cope with even the slightest criticism, extreme sensitivity, and a hunger for attention. Those who suffer from such disorders sometimes find it impossible to hold a job, to attend school, or to sustain relationships. They have low opinions of themselves and judge themselves very critically. They become socially isolated, often by their own choice.

Many people suffer from anorexia nervosa, which is self-induced starvation. Those who are anorexic have difficulty in concentrating, weakness, coldness, and lowered vital signs. It isn't that the victims aren't hungry; they're hungry all the time. They deny themselves food. Weight is lost in a variety of ways: diruetic and laxative use, fasting, endless exercising, diet aids, calorie restriction, and, in some cases, self-induced vomiting.

Following are three stories of recovery. In-patient care is sometimes necessary, as evidenced in the first account.

I was 34 years old and weighed 80 pounds. I had entered the hospital at my husband's insistence and the psychiatrist's recommendation. I didn't think I belonged there. My husband had read about anorexia and knew that I had many symptoms. I was weak and occasionally blacked out.

I was not looking forward to meeting the other anorectics and bulimics. The anorectics starved themselves. The bulimics binged on large amounts of food and then purged what they'd eaten by exercising, starving, or vomiting.

When I arrived, the nurse took my temperature. It was 93 degrees. My blood pressure was 90 over 40. I learned that these are symptoms of anorexia. At home, I had weighed myself 60 or 70 times a day. Now the nurses weighed us each only once a day and made us turn away from the scales.

"What do you eat within a day?" the nurse asked me.

"Luncheon meat," I said.

"A sandwich?" she asked.

"No, just a slice of luncheon meat," I replied.

Later, when they brought the meal trays, I cut my food in tiny pieces and spent a half-hour arranging them on the plate. I also discovered that those with my disease have eating rituals, like eating nothing that is green or consuming no yeast products during Passover or refusing to eat food of animal origin.

In group time, with nervous stomach and dry mouth, I shared my story. I found it was not too different from everyone else's. Whether overweight or underweight, we were all treated with respect. Each of us shared our problems and fears. My greatest fear was that my two little daughters would either hate me or forget me. When they came to my room, they always said, "Please come home, mommy."

Unknown to me, I had entered a treatment and education program that focused beyond mere weight disorders and toward the *real* problems. I learned that the purpose of the program was to build self-esteem, develop proper nutrition, teach us to insist on our rights, and to learn to relax. I also became aware that social isolation is an important factor in the illness.

I spent one and a half months in the hospital. Of course, recovery involves much more than just learning to eat again. As an outpatient, I must keep in touch with the hospital staff. But. I am taking positive steps to recover. I've gotten to the source of the problems. I've learned that I not only want to survive but to live.

It was when Avis entered treatment that she realized the depths of her eating disorder.

Avis Rumney might skip breakfast, eat a salad or sandwich for lunch (but only if she had exercised heavily beforehand), and then skip dinner. This was her typical eating pattern for 17 years of anorexia nervosa. Her obsession with thinness made her feel that, even at 68 pounds, she could still be thinner.

Most of the time, she was too depressed to eat. Antidepressants, therapy, and marriage did not fill her emptiness or provide her with a sense of direction. Food was a reward, and she rarely felt deserving. She viewed her amenorrhea as a convenient form of birth control and her ability to go without food as a way to save money. She refused to acknowledge her eating disorder as a problem. When she eventually entered a treatment program for her depression, she was offended to be diagnosed an as anorexic.

Avis has been at a normal weight for more than nine years. She now enjoys her work, relationships, meals, and time alone. Her perfectionism has been replaced by a quest for personal fulfillment and an ongoing process of self-discovery. She is a marriage, family, and children's counselor, specializing in eating disorders. She is also the author of a book on anorexia nervosa.[8]

Bulimia nervosa consists of binge eating followed by some form of purging (this may take the form of laxative or diuretic abuse, fasting, diet pills, or strenuous exercising). Often the symptoms include depression. Approximately twenty percent of female college students have bulimia nervosa. Four times as many victims suffer from bulimia nervosa as from anorexia nervosa. Those with bulimia may have dental problems, esophagus disorders, constant thirst, extremes in bowel function, heart flutters, and constant sore throats. Some persons see-saw between anorexia and bulimia. Many have recognized their problems, taken a firm hold, and determined to recover.

"Brenda" is one of those individuals. She comments about her dual disorders.

> I've seen depression and despair, also hardship and hopelessness, as a result of an eating disorder. This includes anorexia, bulimia, and compulsive overeating (I've had all three). For years I wanted to die, mainly because of pain caused to myself and others. I didn't think I'd ever be happy again.
>
> Then I took a seminar and learned about love and acceptance. I learned that I'm a worthy, valuable, and worthwhile person. Ever since, I've worked with the challenges life has given me. I've tried to use my eating disorder to my advantage. It's taught me about acceptance of where I am, forgiveness for my wrongdoings, and patience with myself in the process of life. I know that by making one positive choice at a time, I'm building a great life for myself!
>
> (Note: The last time I saw Brenda, she was a beautiful girl of average weight and with much self-confidence.)

Gambling Addiction

Charles Dickens wrote about another addiction that has been around for a long time and takes many forms. In *The Old Curiosity Shop*, the grandfather reveals his passion for gambling, as his grandaughter, Nell, fearfully watches.

> "The gentleman has thought better of it, and isn't coming," said Isaac, making as though he would rise from the table. "I'm sorry the gentleman's daunted—nothing venture, nothing have—but the gentleman knows best."
>
> "Why, I am ready. You have all been slow but me," said the old man. "I wonder who's more anxious to begin than I."
>
> As he spoke, he drew a chair to the table; and the other three closing round it at the same time, the game commenced.
>
> The child sat by, and watched its progress with a troubled mind. Regardless of the run of luck, and mindful only of the desperate passion which had its hold upon her grandfather, losses and gains were to her alike. Exulting in some brief triumph, or cast down by a defeat, there he sat so wild and restless, so feverishly and intensely anxious, so terribly eager, so ravenous for the paltry stakes, that she could have almost better borne to see him dead.[9]

A modern-day "chance-taker," "John," was also wild and restless. He descended into the deceptive world of gambling as a young man. He was the son of a prominent father who had great dreams for "John." His mother was a ridiculing, spiteful woman who made life miserable for her husband and did not help her son's feelings of self-worth either.

"John's" first gambling venture was as a college student. A friend introduced him to gambling. His first efforts ended in disaster. He was broke in a few hours. He did not gamble again for several years. Soon, he began to bet on horses, after carefully studying the racing forms. That, too, proved to be disastrous. He had a good job at the time but was fired because his employer discovered he was much in debt.

He left for Reno, where he went through a succession of wins and losses at the gaming tables. Another good job back home ended in dismissal because he spent too much time at the racetrack. He continued to bet at the track, barely supporting his family with his winnings.

He, then, obtained another job and was very successful at it. But, there was a nagging unhappiness inside him. He returned to Reno to try to shake the depression that plagued him by gambling.

"John" had never been so broke and so far from home before. Time after time people cashed checks for him, not realizing the checks were no good. His stories of bad luck were all lies. Often he was gone from home for months at a time. He made the rounds of the gambling meccas of the west—Tahoe, Las Vegas, Los Angeles, and Reno. His mode of travel was hitchhiking. Once he had a wife, children, car, home, and a good job. Now he was an unshaven vagabond, who wore wrinkled and soiled clothing with cigarette burns.

Going home meant jail or prison. He had left a legacy of bad checks across the country. By now he was emaciated and hollow-eyed. He had constant feelings of loneliness and depression, drowning much of his sorrow in drinking bouts. On the verge of taking his life, "John" sought out a recovering gambler who helped him know how to make restitution.

He was advised to attend support groups for recovering gamblers regularly. His next step was to contact an attorney to write letters promising payment to his creditors.

He called his wife. He was amazed at her coldness. She made no promises of forgiveness or reconciliation. He was gradually able to get a better job. He was allowed to see his wife and children, though he was never able to live with them again.

Slowly, with the help of friends and a support group, "John" had begun his recovery. An amount was set aside to pay all his creditors. Today he helps to support his family. His gambling is a thing of the past. "I've lost much in life, but not everything," he says.

Gambling is a very cunning, deceptive addiction. It begins innocently. One places a bet, wins, and excitedly takes another chance, then another and another. Soon he may be gambling regularly. It may become life-consuming. What begins as a social act can become compulsive. Eventually the gambler starts to lose. Then, he begins the process known as "chasing." He bets more in order to regain the money he has lost.

Treatment for gambling consists of being in a safe environment, which often means an inpatient program. Compulsive gamblers receive therapy among a group of fellow gambling addicts. They begin to change their value systems. In order to regain the values they once had, they must learn to become completely honest. Many have been able to regain their honesty. As part of the treatment, they must repay all the money they owe, regardless how long it takes to do that. They set up a budget to make full restitution. They must also actively continue in a support group.

Gambling has a ravaging effect on individuals. One man said, "My dad left for Las Vegas in a $2,200 Buick. He came back home in a $65,000 Trailways bus."[10]

Sexual Addictions

Compulsive sexual addictions have been treated more extensively in another chapter. Bart Delin's observation, however, is pertinent here.

Sex offenders . . . are not born anti-social; their behavior is learned. Extreme sibling rivalry, lack of love from their families, along with great conflict between their parents themselves, are the prime causes of deviancy. Inner rages, frustrations, and a feeling of self-worthlessness result.[11]

Patrick Carnes has noted,

One of the worst consequences of the addiction is the addicts' *isolation*. The itensity of the double life relates directly to the distance of the addicts from their friends and family. That is, the more intensely involved in compulsive sexual life the addicts become, the more alienated they become from their parents, spouses, and children. Without those human connections, the addicts paradoxically lose touch with their own selves. . . . The addict's world has become totally insulated from real life.[12]

Addicts can and sometimes do recover. Overcomers Outreach reports, "As sexual addiction parallels chemical addictions, so does the pathway of recovery—beginning with an admission of personal powerlessness and unmanageability, in this case over lust."[13]

Though the battle is tough, many people are winning their fight against addictions and finding freedom in a new and better life.

Notes

[1]Thornton Wilder, *Our Town* (1965)

[2]Stanton Peele, *Diseasing of America: Addiction Treatment Out of Control* (New York: Lexington Books, 1989) 31-32.

[3]Ibid.

[4]Lindsey Hall and Leigh Cohn, *Recoveries* (Carlsbad, CA: Gurze Books, 1987) 15.

[5]Ibid., 105.

[6]*It's Up to You* (Chicago: Blue Cross and Blue Shield Association, 1982) 55-57. Used with permission.

[7]Illustration is from the front cover of the pamphlet, *Food, Friend or Foe?* (LaHabra, CA: Overcomers Outreach, Inc., 1990).

[8]Hall and Cohn, 37.

[9]Charles Dickens, *The Old Curiosity Shop* (New York: Viking Penguin, 1943) 223.

[10]Guy Phillips, "Phillips and Company," St Louis, MO: Y-98 FM, 9 July 1992.

[11]Bart Delin, *The Sex Offender* (New York: Beacon Press, 1978).

[12]Patrick Carnes, *Out of the Shadows* (Minneapolis: Compcare Publishers, 1983) 15.

[13]*Sexual Addictions in the Church* (LaHabra, CA: Overcomers Outreach, 1991) 3.

Chapter 8

I Played All the Roles

I realize the path back to sanity and some degree of happiness begins with me and that it won't happen overnight. I have much work to do. I know, too that if my children are to be healthy, I must make it happen. But, that is contingent on me getting healthy first. I have tried to detach from Bill's problem and maybe from him too. I cannot know what our future holds; I don't try to do that anymore.

So writes the wife of an alcoholic. Families of addicted persons live daily with fear, anxiety, pain, and sadness. Living with an addicted spouse is life-shaking. If, for instance, the addicted spouse is the husband, the wife is hurt and upset by repeated drinking episodes. She may be the glue that holds the family together. She is oftentimes the breadwinner. She may see the only solution as separation or divorce. But this only increases her sense of failure. She brings to the marriage: resentment, anger, fear, hurt, and hostility. Sometimes the non-addicted spouse tries to absorb all the pain like a blotter to keep the rest of the family from knowing and suffering. Her over-involvement with the chemical dependent takes her time, energy, money, and her own interests and goals.

Living with an Alcoholic Spouse

It was true of "Rachel." She could not look forward to the future. In fact, it was her greatest fear.

At the age of 32, I was diagnosed with cancer. That day in the doctor's office I stood at the window, staring in disbelief. Was this really happening? What would become of my children if they were left to be reared by their father? Three weeks after my diagnosis, I had surgery to remove the cancer.

Two and a half years later, after 15 years of marriage, my husband came home from work, packed a few clothes, and told me he needed to get away for a couple of weeks so he "could think." He never returned. His drinking had been a source of many conflicts over the years. The last few months preceding this night had been especially bad.

This relationship had been a destructive one, but it was all I knew. I knew how to act and react. I had done this far too long. His leaving me left me devastated. The children were deeply hurt and confused. I was extremely angry at him for placing me in a position I never wanted.

I had stereotyped divorced women before. Now, I was about to become one more statistic. I was deeply humbled. Being filled with shame and embarrassment prevented me from telling friends what had happened. My children and my job forced me to keep going through the daily routines. In fact, these two things may have saved my life.

Every day, after coming home from work, I shut myself in the closet, sat on the floor and cried. I found myself entertaining suicidal thoughts. My despair was like a deep, black, bottomless chasm. After about two months, I sought counseling and a support group. I remained in counseling and the support group for two years.

I was very fortunate to have good health and a secure job. At least, I could support myself and the kids. My budget was stretched to the limit and then some. But God faithfully provided for my daily needs.

Five and a half years after my divorce, I met a man who, I felt, was an answer to my prayer. Don't get me wrong. I had not prayed for a man. Not me! Darryl and I met on a blind date set up by mutual friends. I saw this as an opportunity for a free meal—nothing more.

Neither of us wowed each other when we met. We just made the best of the evening. As time went on, though, we discussed marriage. I loved this man, and it was with a heavy heart that I sought out God's will. The thought of re-marrying was a very scary one. After a few weeks, I noticed I was feeling more peaceful about the situation. In time, we were married.

Because I have been given much, I too must give to whomever needs my help. I must accept those persons where they are.

Rachel has shown it clearly. The alcoholic himself is the actor—others react to what he does. He drinks to take away his loneliness, relieve all his pain, take away his tensions, solve all his problems, and to boost his well-being and self-sufficiency. He steadfastly denies that his drinking is causing him trouble. But he is aware of the fact that he is a failure. When the family protects and shares in his delusions, he steadily declines. Everyone in the family knows what everyone pretends not to know. These lies keep the family frozen in helplessness. There is no chance that the addicted one will stop his addiction unless he is made to face the consequences. Many spouses awaken every day—to fear.

Living with a Gambling Addict

Addictions other than alcoholism plague the family structure. The wife of a gambler tells of her slow recovery.

Whenever "Paul" called, there were always promises to "come home as soon as I take care of the debts." With the births of each of our two children, we were very happy. Always, however, "Paul" returned to his addiction.

We feared he was dead somewhere when we didn't hear from him for long periods at a time. Our oldest child was devastated because he had been very close to his father.

Even when my husband came back home and promised to make restitution, I found I couldn't believe him. I had struggled with trying to be a mother and father, with supporting the family by myself. I was finally determined to live without him. I didn't want him to hurt me or the children anymore. It had already had a marked effect on the oldest child, who was sad and withdrawn. There seemed to be nothing I could do to make him happy. He took adult burdens on his young shoulders and worried about what would happen to our family.

The last time my husband came back promising restitution, I knew that if I forgave him, it meant more chance-taking. He could leave us again. We had not seen him for months. Rather than depend on his recovery for my happiness, I refused to take him back. I decided to get help for myself instead. I sought recovery through counseling and support groups. My husband

and I have never reconciled. The children and I have accepted it, however, and healing is taking place in our lives.

Parents of Addicts

In addition to the addictions that must be dealt with by spouses, many parents find themselves dealing with the addiction of their child. It is a shattering experience to see one's hopes and dreams for that child disintegrate. Many parents refuse to talk about a "lost child" in the family. Out of courtesy, friends cease to ask about the child. But, the pain of the parents is still there and buried deep inside. Often, parents find that many of their ideas of parenting must change.

One parent said:

> Toughlove *is* tough when you must act differently than you ever have. When you must go to the police to turn in your kid. Or when you go to neighbors and friends to tell them about your child's outrageous behavior and ask their support. Or when you change what "good" and "bad" parenting always meant to you. Or when you ask school officials, police, social workers, and judges to help you control your own offspring. Or when you stand up in court and tell the judge you know your son is guilty. Or when you and your group take your kid to a detoxification center against her will. Or when you tell your daughter she cannot drive the family car because she is a drunk. Or when you fear that your wayward daughter is back on barbiturates but you refuse to take her home without her going to a drug rehab. Or when you tell your oldest son he has to move out of the house. Or when your kid is living in a car and you avoid contacting him.[1]

The "whys" of an addicted child's rebellion are not always clear. A mother tells of her confusion. Eventually she understood the why's of her son's behavior. The whole family is recovering. She also discovered *Toughlove.*

> I was very involved in school. I was a member of the PTA, a room mother, and a volunteer for everything. I thought this was the way to stay in touch with my children. I have two sons, three years apart. So when Kevin was in high school, I became very involved in PTA Teachers' Appreciation, newsletters, the works.

You see I was helping to bring a word about "drugs" to parents through the newsletters.

Our older son, Kevin, was involved heavily in sports, chorus, and clubs, and in making good grades. The younger son, Scott, was back there in Junior High, not too much going, or so I thought. Of course, he found a pastime. It was alcohol. Even though we never pushed Scott, except for better grades, he always felt he was competing with Kevin. Scott needed attention in the worst way, but I didn't see it. So, while I was busy with Kevin, our youngest was getting more heavily into alcohol.

Scott would come home with cuts and scratches. He would explain that he had fallen down an embankment on his bike. The next time he would have a flat tire and fall from his bike. I never stopped to think, "This boy never had this problem before." Every weekend he was banged up.

No lights had gone off in our heads yet. We needed a "jolt." It came. Scott passed out on the road to our house. Some people stopped to help him. Some of his friends came along, intervened, and brought him home. I found him some hours later passed out on the bathroom floor—cut, bruised, and dirty. He had thrown-up. The light was beginning to go on. Could this boy have a problem? My husband assured me boys do things like this. He had done it as a teenager. "Scott will be all right," he assured me. But, I couldn't let go of the thought that our son was in trouble.

I kept hearing how addicted kids pick up new friends and change habits. His friends had not changed—he had. I was pleading with him to stop running around with those boys, telling him that they were a bad influence. Much later, in counseling, Scott let me know that *he* was the one who was the bad influence on his friends.

We were all sick and didn't know it. We needed help, which took almost two years. Scott was driving by this time, having wrecks, losing his license, in trouble at school, and in trouble with the police. We got him into counseling first. Then, he entered a hospital for rehabilitation. He was there for 38 days.

The second time in treatment, a year later, he was in for 11 days. We were in counseling for years, also in parents' support groups and aftercare. The hospital experience was our best education. I learned so much about myself, my husband, and our sons. Counseling, family support groups, and the grace of God saved us.

This thing can grab our family again. We are always on the lookout for that "old stinking thinking" that lets us know something's not right. This means we need to talk, do some digging, and find out what's going on. We must try not to let him bury his feelings. If that won't work, we back off and let the chips fall where they may. He knows, and we know, that we can't do it for him. We're not going to be bloodhounds. Backing away has been good for all of us. I got in too deeply. I lived this thing 24 hours a day. I was missing out on a balanced life. But, at least, for now, our son is recovering and doing well. So are we.

"Fred" indicates the intensity of emotions that parents with an addicted child often feel.

I have heard it said that recovery begins by "letting go." Letting go of what? Does it mean I should stop loving him? Never. Stop caring? No. It's so confusing! What are we to do? When will his pain, and ours, end? *Will* it end? How? By his suicide? By violent confrontation or accident? By all of us going mad (can we take much more of this, or are we going to snap?) Or, will we live as bitter prisoners, chained to his emotional state, desperate for escape (but not knowing how)?

Sometimes I am calm and assured, believing "he's doing pretty good!" The next moment, abruptly face-to-face with some new crisis, I stand in shock trying to assess how to respond and cope.

I never dreamed this would happen. But who does? To recover, one must deal with shock, confusion, paralysis, anger, and control. Each takes its turn.

"Otto" expresses some of the same emotions.

My wife and I had three children. I played all the roles. We divorced after 16 years, just about the time our oldest son, who is a chemical dependent, started to become incorrigible and destructive. We couldn't believe that one of our children was an alcoholic and a drug abuser. After doing everything we could think of, guess, or dream of, we discovered nothing helped. We placed him in a treatment center and participated in their family program. After 50 days, he came out some better. It wasn't long, though, before he went back to his addictions.

I was still ignorant, not understanding his problems or how to deal with them. His mother got a restraining order and threw him out of the house. I was in agreement. He was 19. Over the next several years, he moved around. He lived with his maternal grandparents until they threw him out. He lived in his car, moved in with me, left, moved around awhile, then asked if he could move in with me again. I said "No."

He had exhausted his family's emotional resources. The debris of damaged family emotions and feelings lay scattered about among the destroyed cars, windows, doors, walls, and furniture. The effects of alcohol and drug abuse are devastating. I knew he was hurting badly and having a terrible time of it. Often, I didn't even know where he was.

In recent years, our son has cleaned up his act, gotten a job, and arrested his addictions. He is now doing well in college. I'm proud of his new accomplishments, sorry about what he went through, and thankful for the future.

Like Otto, other parents have faced similar disappointments, followed later by much gratification.

"By all appearances, it looks like he is going to make it," says "Frank" of his son.

My son was not well. He changed from being the (mostly) obedient boy whom I thought I knew well, to an emotionally explosive—and sometimes violent—stranger. "No," he said, "I don't drink or do drugs, and I'll be okay." I believed him. He was so convincing, I wanted to believe him. Sometimes he looked good—active, interested, full of plans. At other times he was sullen, and reclusive. But wasn't every teenager moody at times? Didn't they demand privacy?

I knew the divorce was not easy on him. I knew he had problems with his néw stepfather. I knew how he cried when I remarried. Still, counseling seemed to help. I was there for him. We all were. We all loved him. He would be okay. Surely he would. It amazes me, now, to realize how reality can be obscured and for so long.

Even now, the task of writing brings back flashes of frightening experiences. Helplessly rocking my grown son in my lap as he mumbled "Daddy," the desire for life ebbing from his stupored body. Grappling with him on the floor, thrown about like a rag doll, until medics and police could subdue his rage. Rushing home from work in response to my wife's frantic call. He was unconscious and unresponsive. Was he alive or dying, poisoned by some unknown overdose, I wondered.

I was as unable to control my son's recovery from chemical dependency as I would be to control his recovery from a malignancy or any other type of potentially fatal disease. I needed to recognize and confront the problems. I needed to reach out to others—counselors, doctors, clergy, family, and friends—for the tools, assistance and support they could provide. I could practice the so-called "Toughlove," by letting my son accept the natural consequences of his actions.

Recovery, for him and for us, has not been easy. My son is making solid strides. By all appearances, it looks like he is going to make it. My wife and I have managed to "detach"—as the saying goes. We have had to accomplish this state for our own sanity and survival. We have taken the steps we can take. But we also recognize that our son's recovery is now his to make.

Addictions Effects on the Family System

A pamphlet provided by the Houston Council on Alcoholism and Drug abuse makes a point about the larger effects of addiction within a family.

> When Junior gets the flu, no one is surprised when his sisters and brothers, and Mom and Dad as well, come down with the illness. But it may surprise you to learn that when someone is an alcoholic, the effects of the illness show up in other family members as well. . . . Behavioral patterns for different family members are developed as a way of coping with the painful and difficult problem of alcohol addiction. Without help, they may persist. . . . For this reason, family treatment programs, as well as support groups . . . are of benefit.[2]

The pamphlet also identifies the "roles" that family members take on. These are listed below. You will observe that what is seen on the outside is not what those persons feel on the inside.

Victim (the chemical dependent)
    Outside: Hostility, manipulation, aggression, rigid values, charm
    Inside: Shame, guilt, fear, pain, hurt

Family Hero (caretaker of the family)
    Outside: Good kid, high achiever, follows rules, seeks approval, very responsible
    Inside: Guilt, hurt, inadequacy

Mascot (the family clown)
    Outside: Immature, fragile, cute, hyperactive, distracting
    Inside: Fear, anxiety, insecurity

Chief Enabler (Closest emotionally to victim, protector of family)
    Outside: Self-righteous, super-responsible, sarcastic, passive, physically sick, martyr
    Inside: Anger, hurt, guilt, low self-esteem

Scapegoat (problem child)
    Outside: Hostile, defiant, rule breaker, in trouble
    Inside: Rejection, hurt, guilt, jealousy, anger

Lost Child (the forgotten child in the family)
    Outside: Shy, quiet, fantasy life, solitary, mediocre, attaches to things, not people
    Inside: Rejection, hurt, anxiety[3]

As a result of taking on roles, family members are not "real" people. They may even switch roles from time to time.

It's hard to believe the lies that are told, the stories that are manufactured, when spouses and children try to cover their addictions. Their goal becomes one of throwing family members "off track." The family members who love them believe those stories. The survival of the family depends on the recovery of each member. Otherwise, society may very well see the fragmentation of that family.

Notes

[1]Phyliss York, David York, and Ted Wachtel, *Toughlove* (New York: Doubleday, 11982) 136.

[2]*Alcoholism, the Family Illness* (Houston, TX: Houston Council on Alcoholism and Drug Abuse, 1987).

[3]Ibid. The "roles" given here were originally defined by Sharon Wegscheider-Cruse.

Chapter 9

The Deep, Dark Pit

It was almost the first news we heard as we de-planed. Our twenty-year-old son, Matt, had come to pick us up at the airport. "I've bought a dog," he said, "she won't get really big, she's a Lab. Her name is Sam, short for Samantha." My heart sank. I remembered his cat, Patches, now departed. Until the day of her demise, I did *everything* for her.

Time proved Matt's prediction wrong. Sam did get big. She dug holes in the yard, wrecked the flowers, tore a hole in the screen to the sunporch, crawled in and chewed up the cushions. We built a smaller, separate, fenced-in area for her in the back yard. In no time, she was over the fence and into the bigger yard again. I carried groceries in through the front door, avoiding the back door entirely. I tiptoed down the driveway to keep her from waking and barking early in the morning.

Very early one morning, I looked out the window to see chrysanthemums, which my husband, Bob, had planned to plant, scattered around the back yard. "Heaven help us all," I thought. "This is the last straw." I put Sam back into the "dog yard," as Bob referred to her "digs." I picked up pieces of chrysanthemums and stuffed them into pots. As I climbed back into bed for awhile, I heard the merciful sound of heavy rain. It was the perfect cover-up for the crime, I thought. It didn't work. I hadn't been able to hide all the evidence.

"Something has to be done," I said. "If I didn't love her so much, I would just get rid of her," said Matt. (Sam did have the most soulful eyes). Nevertheless, this was major conflict.

Forty-eight feet of lawn edging and 140 feet of steel wire later, Matt and I stood back to admire our work on the "dog yard." It looked like a concentration camp. Sam and I eyeballed each other through the fence. "We've got you now," I said. That evening I went out onto the sunporch and there she sat. One hundred fifty more feet of steel wire later, she was still outward bound. I had begun to call it the "Surviving Sam Syndrome."

Sam left us when our son went back to college, but I won't forget her. She taught me something about life. Just when you think it's secure, you discover that it isn't. No amount of preparation can fortify us against crises that come. At any moment, we can come crashing down from our perch of protection. To whom or what will we turn when it happens? The insecurities of life can sometimes lead to deep depression and other emotional illnesses.

Happy people can accept life's whole package of joy, sadness, laughter, tears, pain, and exhiliration. Most of us find happiness in something outside ourselves. But self-pity can destroy us. Adjusting oneself to "what is" is one of the difficult facets of life. If a child does not learn to accept disappointment early in life, he cannot adjust to "what is" in adulthood.

Struggling with Depression

"Melissa" had trouble adjusting because she was having a difficult struggle with depression. With the support of others, she found ways to cope and deal with her circumstances.

On February 17, 1989, my husband passed away after suffering with cancer for six years. June 28, 1989, my mother, who lived with us, passed away with a major heart attack. Then, on July 1, 1989, my son moved away to work in another city. In between the two deaths, I retired from my teaching job. My world came down.

To cope with being alone that first year, I "ran away." I took tours to Wisconsin and the eastern states to see the fall colors. I also flew to Florida to visit my sister for several weeks. On the first anniversary of my husband's death, I "ran away" again by going to Hawaii. As long as I was gone or with people, I felt great. When I had to come home, however, I was very depressed.

All I wanted to do was cry, sleep, and eat. I knew I couldn't do that, so I called on someone I knew who could and would help me, my pastor. After talking to me, he realized I needed more help than he could give. He suggested I see a psychiatrist. With my permission, he made an appointment for me. I took an anti-depressant medicine that helped me feel well enough to get out of bed each morning, get dressed, and fix breakfast.

After stopping the medicine, I still had bad times, especially in the evenings and on Saturday—the worst day of the week. I knew I had to go on with my life, so I found things to occupy my time. I started taking an oil painting class and piano lessons, which I had wanted to do for a long time. Also, I volunteered to work with internationals, which helped during the week. But, then came Saturdays, which, even today, are still very hard to get through.

Now I have made some new friends who have lost their husbands. We go out for dinner each Friday evening. That helps a lot because Friday is still another bad evening. Our widows' support group, friends, and a puppy are helping me. But after two and a half years, I still do not like evenings and Saturdays. I'm doing less crying, and I pray that each day will get better. I even talk out loud to God when things seem to be going wrong.

I know I must go on. My husband and mother would want me to do this. With God's help, I will recover.

Overcoming the Darkness

Many people who have gone through periods of deep sadness have fought to rise above it. Ida Nelle Holloway suffered with severe depression for many years. About her autobiography, *When All the Bridges Are Down*, she said:

> For a long time I just had to try to keep believing there was still a light at the end of the long, dark tunnel. Little by little, that light became a reality. Now, even though I sometimes lose sight of it momentarily, I no longer doubt it is there. The joy this confidence brings makes me long to share it with others.[1]

Continued sadness and dejection can take much of the balance out of life. Anna Campbell has commented on the extremism often found in depressed persons.

> Depressed people often set standards that are too high for themselves. They are never pleased with their own accomplishments, resulting in low self-esteem. They are tolerant of the shortcomings in others that they would not tolerate in themselves. People who are depression-prone are inclined to very readily "own" their failures ("it was my fault," etc.),

which feeds into their negative sense of self-esteem. But they are inclined not to "own" their successes ("It was just luck," etc.). Persons more resistant to depression tend to forget about or even distort their failures. and *remember their successes*. It is important to be able to develop a solid, well-earned legitimate sense of our own worthwhileness.[2]

When we feel that we cannot control some significant aspect of our lives, it increases the likelihood of depression." "Judy" knew that her life was out of control.

Only once in my life have I been severely depressed. It was a time when I could not control my circumstances. It was the blackest blackness I have every known. I felt as if I were in a deep, dark pit, unable to climb out. I can remember crying out to no one in particular, "Help me." I felt heavy-hearted, as if someone were actually sitting on my chest.

Yes, I thought of suicide. Most people do when confronted with feelings of great hopelessness. It's no "crime" to think about it. It's no sign of weakness. But I knew I must get help and get it quickly.

I sought counseling. Slowly, slowly, I began to climb out of the darkness. It was like turning on a bright light in a dark room.

I won't forget that time in my life and the horror of it. I felt it was worse than a physical illness. Interestingly enough, I've never been that depressed since. I think that I'm just determined never to be that sad again. When I have unhappy, depressing thoughts, I start to think happy thoughts. I also read from the book of Psalms in the Bible. I find great comfort there.

The Depths of Depression

Others battle low spirits also, but find ways to compensate. For "Anne," the depths of depression have been many. She was born shortly before the Great Depression of the 1930s. She was reared by a widowed mother who felt much pain and loneliness after the loss of her spouse and the lack of the where-with-all to raise two daughters. "Anne" grew to womanhood, married "Joe," a very wonderful, gentle man, who has provided for her well. They raised five beautiful children.

Their first-born, "Bill," was a beautiful baby; he was intelligent and so loved by them. In the early years, the young family was relocated several times due to "Joe's" occupation. The moves took their toll and "Bill" seemed illness-prone and unable to cultivate lasting friendships. He graduated from college, even though his goals did not seem too firmly established. A year after graduation, he married. From early on, it appeared the couple was insecure and floundering. After nine years, the marriage was dissolved, and the mother was given custody of the children, a daughter and a son. It was not a good situation. The children were later removed from the home by child-care authorities. Neglect and chemical dependency were given as reasons for the removal.

"Anne" and "Joe" were asked to care for the children for a period of three weeks. The time extended into seven and a half years, during which time the children seemed to flourish. Unfortunately, due to fetal alcohol syndrome, constant exposure to smoking, and lack of a proper diet during the pregnancies, the children were judged to be developmentally handicapped. This meant special classes in school and much frustration for the grandparents.

"Bill" had a job at the time of the divorce. He did not have enough income to pay for child care, however, nor did he have the ability to raise the children alone. Many times "Bill's" whereabouts were unknown to his parents for as long as a year. "Bill," lived in shelters and substandard housing. He has received much professional counseling and group therapy. But, he has never seemed to get to the grass roots of the real problems.

Once "Anne" was so sad over not knowing whether "Bill" was dead or alive, she went to a downtown mission to inquire whether they had seen "Bill" or fed him. A minister there definitely did know her son. He told her how "Bill" had wept over not being able to follow in his father's footsteps. "Joe" had never leveled such expectations upon his son. His parents had just just hoped that "Bill" could get some kind of gainful employment to keep his own body and soul together and to help provide for his two deserving children.

"Bill's" future looks bleak. On the plus side, many doors have opened to the children as a result of professional counseling and medical aid to help them deal with their handicaps. In the meantime, "Joe" and "Anne" pray that solutions can be arrived at and all will have a happy ending. They are finding other things to be joyful about.

A young man shares some secrets of his illness. "Dan" suffered from deep depression, stress anxiety, confusion, and frustration for many years. He says the term "depression" can be a convenient umbrella term. This is the way he tells his story.

> My first experience of a major nature involved being so angry because my family, whom I loved and trusted, no longer trusted me. I was accused of sexually abusing my own daughter. Nothing was further from my mind when, as a parent, I spent time playing with both children. I was angry that I was accused by people whom I loved. I was upset. When I sought help from the psychiatrist and psychologist, I was asked questions about depression. "Don't you feel depressed? Don't you feel like committing suicide?" What I was feeling was anger at having no control over what other people do.
>
> My second experience involved seeking help "to re-establish control over my own life." I don't have much authority over what I want to do. I have even less influence over what others choose for me to do. Again, I was angry that I allowed others to rule what I did or didn't do. I resolved to exercise more control over my own reactions to what others do. I haven't always succeeded. But, I continually strengthen my resolve to try harder.

Joanna suffered a more severe loss of command over her own life. She details her sadness. It began in childhood.

> Some of us don't even know that we are in pain and depression until a host of friends who care tell us that we are. When we accept their caring, we take the first step on our journey toward wellness.
>
> In my childhood, in our house, you did as you were told or you were beaten within an inch of your life. You were slapped everywhere my father's hand could reach or whipped with a paddle until it broke in two. Your legs were striped with switch marks that cut so deeply that you wore the cuts and their scars afterward to school for weeks at a time. Dad hit us if we did not

answer him on the first call as we played in neighbors' yards. He hit us if we did not eat lunch and dinner in fifteen minutes. He hit us if he were tired or in a bad mood as a result of something that had happened at his job that day. His blows bruised us and made us bleed. No amount of make-up could cover them, though we tried.

What my father said, we did. There was no such thing as an option in our house. Might made right. It also made children who trusted only their mother. It made children who could have only very limited friendships because they were not allowed to have their classmates over to visit. Unfortunately, it made children who were totally without a knowledge of who they were as people.

My mother died of a sudden heart attack in December, 1990, three days before Christmas. When my mother died, a part of me died, too. In February, 1991, my father died unexpectedly of an accident that happened in the hospital during a routine biopsy procedure. Six weeks before my dad died, my sister and her children found my brother-in-law who had hanged himself in his home. In fourteen months, I lost both my parents, my brother-in-law, my gentle collie dog, Margaret, and I lost my rapport with my sister. We had been more like strangers to each other at Dad's funeral than sisters—neither of us seeing each other's need.

In meetings and support groups, I have learned that our family's problems are shared by others. I have discovered that there are people who—because they have been wounded themselves—are patient listeners and helpful supporters. All of these companions have fed my spirit. My support groups have put me in touch with friends who are "safe." Gradually old walls are coming down. New doors are being opened.

When we receive support and therapy, we hear glad music and the wonderful laughter of our friends enjoying a celebration. It tantalizes us and we yearn for it. "There it is," we say with arm outstretched and finger pointed. "That's the *me* I want to be." We want inside. We want to be at home with ourselves.

Circumstances in our lives may sadden us, but climbing out of the deep, dark pit is even more difficult for those who suffer mental and emotional illnesses. One serious form of mental disorder is manic-depressive illness, a malady that one would not wish on anyone. Recovery is difficult.

David Wogoder makes an observation, though, worth considering:

> But, it is worth recalling that there is another and more positive side to the ailment that is sometimes overlooked. A surprising proportion of the world's most creative and original individuals have suffered from manic-depressive illness; and some would certainly have said that their sufferings were more than compensated by their creative gifts. Recent studies have shown that manic-depressive illness is particularly common amongst poets. The list includes John Clare, William Cowper, Edgar Allan Poe, Robert Lowell, John Berryman, and many others.[5]

Also, as we look back across the pages of history, we see those who probably suffered from it and were never aware of it. All society knew was that they were difficult, if not impossible, people. A victim may be bi-polar, meaning that he is both manic and depressive, or uni-polar, meaning that he is one or the other.

Many are recovering from its dread control over their lives. "Angelica" is one of these.

> When asked to write my story about manic-depressive illness, I was flattered. But, as I think about it, it is very difficult for me to do. This illness has brought me a great deal of pain, loss and separation. These are the adjectives I use to explain MDI: disaster, chaos, confusion, hopelessness, loneliness, desperation, broken relationships, loss, rejection, wanting to accomplish but never able, instability, non-acceptance, and hurt.
>
> When I sit down to write, it forces me to face a lot of things I have never admitted and would like to leave in the past. I am forced to deal with my actions. In the past, when people told me I was unpredicatable, I used to enjoy that. But as my illness has progressed, it's scary. I don't seem to have control over this "unpredictable" life I live.
>
> My friends always think of me as a nice, friendly person, but the friendships always end because of me. I become revengeful. I have hurt a lot of people. I have "used" people a lot, because I can't "do" for myself. I've always felt I live a boring life.
>
> I remember a time when I was dating a member of an outlaw motorcycle club and loving it. I had power, I was looked up to, and for the first time I felt accepted. I didn't realize how dangerous it was to me and to my children.

In the manic stage of the illness, I have energy; I feel I can get things accomplished. But, without medication, I can't deal with the problems my manic state causes. In my depressive state, I wish for dark sleep. I "wish the depression away," but that only makes it worse. I try to stay employed, but I can't. Without medication, I feel so physically "down" I can't get out of bed; I can't get to work. I have a short attention span, and it takes excitement to keep my attention. My judgment is altered—I don't think or care about outcomes, I can always deal with that later. The depression makes me feel that "I don't care anymore."

I have suffered so many losses—homes, cars, personal possessions, and the greatest of all—the loss of my children. I have tried to take my own life, but, for some reason, I'm still here.

Several years ago, my life was full of chaos. I entered a hospital to have the problem diagnosed. Now I must take medication and be in therapy. I will have to deal with it all my life. This is something that will not go away, no matter how I deny it. But now, with a diagnosis, I am learning to accept and to live with the disorder.

The Path toward Recovery

Patients who are manic depressive are usually treated with Lithium Carbonate, a salt used to control mood swings, or a similar medication. If faithful to the medication, they can definitely see improvement.

Symptoms of the illness include:

On the "high" side:
 Elated mood, supercharged energy
 Overspending, foolish business investments
 Increased sexual behavior
 Poor judgment
 Feelings of grandiosity
 Rapid and excessive speech
 Overly argumentative, impulsive
 Rapid, unpredictable emotional changes
 Minimal sleeping

On the "low" side:
   Fatigue, staleness
   Sleep disturbance or sleeping too much
   Hopelessness, helplessness, worthlessness
   Suicidal thoughts
   Inability to make even the smallest decisions
   Sense of impending disaster and doom
   Difficulty concentrating or remembering

Manic depression is not a pleasant disorder with which to live. The illness is very fragmentary to families. The loved ones of the victim must deal with an ailment they do not understand and with which they have little patience. Frustration runs rampant as bizarre behavior continues. Not only the victim, but the victim's family, must fight for survival.

Like a boat tossed by heavy waves, "Dana's" family sought peace and calm from the problems.

I can't say when our son's problems with manic depressive illness really began. As a teenager, he was difficult to control and often obnoxious. He was promiscuous and chose to abandon our moral values. He seemed to have no inhibitions and, in fact, prided himself on his unchaste behavior. Yet, he seemed socially isolated. He lied to us many times. He could not manage money. He was arrested for shoplifting.

When frustrated, he showed hostility, withdrawal, and suspicion. He married a woman who appeared to be emotionally stable. When their children came along, it was obvious that he could not deal with parenthood. Once he walked out of his home and was not heard from for a week. His wife and children were in tears. He suddenly reappeared and acted as if nothing had happened.

The marriage failed, partially because of his financial problems. His spending patterns were not unlike those of a chemical dependent or a gambler. He could not establish priorities with money. If he owed rent money, he went on a spending spree instead. Many times we contributed to his family's financial needs until we realized we were being lied to and manipulated. Our financial aid stopped, which led to much anger on his part. His many debts kept the creditors at his door. As a "single again," his promiscuity returned. When confronted with his problems, he glossed over them, refusing to listen or talk about them.

His ideas were bizarre. He seemed to make enemies and then to feel sorry for himself because he had few friends. He loved to embarrass others in the family in social settings. His unpredictable behavior isolated him from the rest of the family. Then, he went into long tirades about how he "didn't belong." It was obvious that our son was lonely, dejected, and miserable.

At times, he could be jovial and fun-loving. He often talked non-stop. He could be genial and sociable, with humor and good spirits. He could be lavish in his giving to others.

He did complain over and over of physical illness and of being unable to sleep. He was able to get jobs, but was unable to keep them. During his depressed state, he could not get out of bed in the mornings.

Our son hit bottom when he began drinking alcohol. He spent a month in the hospital, where he was diagnosed as manic-depressive. He was given medication, which he continues to take. His condition must be closely monitored. His extreme moods of high and low have evened out, though they have not disappeared.

Though change is slow, our son appears to be recovering. He attends support group meetings and reads a great deal about the illness. He is in a new marriage and shows signs of making new beginnings.

Once recovery is in place, those who are determined to survive the "deep, dark pit" often become very pleasant people with whom to live.

Notes

[1] Ida Nelle Hollaway, *When All the Bridges Are Down* (Nashville: Broadman Press, 1975). From the dust jacket back cover.

[2] From a speech by Anna Campbell. Recorded by Steffie Bova, DMA News, February 1989.

[3] David Wigoder, *Images of Destruction* (London & New York: Routledge & Kegan Paul, 1987) foreword.

Chapter 10

Chuck Had
a Host of Friends

The funeral home had a "special" on funerals. My mother read about it in the newspaper. Planned ahead of time, one could not only save money but "spare your loved ones the grief of planning your funeral while in shock."

Mother called my sister, Mary, and me. "I think it's time to take care of this," she said. We agreed. We arrived at the funeral home. We looked at coffins. "Now, I'd like to see what you have in the back room," she said. (Having lived through the Great Depression, she would not take anything at the first quoted price. She didn't realize that cheaper is not always better. Many times my sisters and I had groaned at being asked to wait while she found something that cost less.)

Having chosen the coffin, we sat down with the director to plan the funeral itself. She carefully thought out the songs and scriptures she most wanted. Then the director said, "Here's the good news, Mrs. Rickerson. If you are in another city when you die, we will fly your body back here for burial"—to which Mother replied in all seriousness, "But I'm afraid to fly." "Mother," said Mary and I in chorus, "you'll be dead!"

I'll never forget her innocent humor. I'm hoping that the memory of that moment will help me to get through the sadness of her funeral and the painful days afterward.

The death of a loved one can be the most damaging experience of our entire lives. Whether expected or unexpected at the time, the shock leaves us emotionally maimed and critically wounded. Perhaps our own wish to die is greatest at that time, because the death of a loved one seems so final. Even those of us who believe in an afterlife find ourselves asking, "When will I see him/her again?" and "What kind of relationship will it be?"

Dealing with Death

Recovery from a death is slow and heart-wrenching. Marcella has found support in dealing with her husband's death.

"Time heals!" so they say. "But not completely," I add. When a loved one dies, the void remains and remains and remains. The truth is that time helps you to adjust.

The shock of the sudden death of my husband carried me through the planning of, and actual participation in, the funeral service. The demands of facing and planning for the immediate future also kept me "afloat" and out of touch with the reality of aloneness. Not until two months later, upon returning from a vacation that took me to familiar people and places, did I finally hit "bottom." For the first time in my life, I truly wanted to die.

Night was the most difficult time. I stayed up as late as possible. But still, when the lights were out, reality had to be faced. I was alone. This was to be a reality for the rest of my life.

Offers of help are often empty. The words I most ignore are, "Call me if you need anything." The young minister who followed in my husband's position and still lives in the area, however, went a step further. Taking me by the arm and looking me in the eye, he asked, "Did you hear me? I mean it! Call me when you need something done." He is the one I call.

In the fall of 1989, twelve and a half years after the death of my husband, my pastor asked me to assist in beginning a support group for widows in our church. Several recently widowed ladies in our membership were having great difficulties facing life alone.

Although our ages and everyday interests vary considerably, through our monthly meetings, we have bonded together in friendship and support. Our fellowship is not limited to our meetings. We also share other social times together. At our meetings, there are times of joy and laughter, as well as times of tears, sadness, and even depression. All emotional expressions are acceptable and met with empathy, whether or not they are understood. Although my function with this group was to help others, I have come to know more fully that healing is a continuous process. I, too, have been helped.

Fourteen years have passed since my husband's death. The widow's support group has helped me to express my feelings and face the facts of widowhood. Having loving, understanding children and grandchildren has also been helpful. It has given me a reason for living.

"Elizabeth" experienced many of the same emotions.

In June, my husband was not feeling well. We had plans to visit our son and his family in a distant state. While on this trip, they took us to see where my husband worked before our marriage. It was a dream come true for him to see this area again.

On returning home, he saw his doctor. The doctor did not find anything that seemed serious. In October, he went fishing with a friend. That night he began suffering with pain in his abdomen. For the next two and one half months, he was x-rayed and examined by other doctors. Finally, early in January, we went to a very fine hospital in another city. After 10 days of x-ray, he was turned over to kidney specialists. A very fine surgeon performed the surgery, which disclosed one of his kidneys completely consumed by cancer. After the surgery, the doctor told my children and me that it was a rare type of cancer that would spread like wildfire. My husband refused to go through chemotherapy.

On February 1, I brought him home. One of my sisters, who had stayed with me all the time we were at the hospital and was such a help to me and to my husband, came home with us. She stayed with us until his death in May. I was able to care for him in our home as long as he lived, which pleased him.

We tried to make the best of every day we had left to be together. He was a kind, loving, and gentle person. He took his suffering silently. We had a wonderful marriage for more than 46 years.

When his demise came, I was devastated. I knew I had to face life alone. My children lived miles away and had their own families. In the presence of other people, I was brave. When I was alone, I wept and cried aloud. I had always loved him so much. I knew he loved me.

Now, I am glad that I can still drive my car, take care of the house and surroundings, and engage in many activities in the community.

The Surviving Spouse and Children

Some of those who grieve have been left to rear children alone.

A knock at the door! My husband's lawyer friend was standing there. He said, "Clynn, Truett had a little heart attack while giving the final argument of the legal case he was involved with at the courthouse. He's in the hospital in Shreveport. I'm here to drive you over." (The trip was 75 miles.)

Our pastor and his wife called to say they were going with me. Was it that serious? I was sure it was minor. But the speed we made caused me to wonder.

The heart attack turned out to be a cerebral hemorrhage. The most damaging part of the attack came two days later. Truett died the following day without realizing his condition. Having been married for only two years, it was indeed a shock. Truett had three children, ages 13, 11, and 7. He and I had a little girl, 10 months. Suddenly, the four were mine to rear without a father. I had to depend on God. Who else could help me?

Friends, family, and community offered full support. They gave their love freely, and their affirmation and assistance came day by day.

Two days after the funeral, a doctor's checkup revealed that I was pregnant (which I had suspected). Seven months later, our son arrived. People rejoiced with us. Then a woeful surprise came. Louisiana law declared the three children's grandfather as guardian of the children. This would cause a breakup of the family. Much interaction occurred trying to keep the family together. Finally, the grandfather gave the guardianship to me. It was a great Thanksgiving season.

I accepted a half-time position as director of a church's weekday program for children. The position lasted five years, until the last child was ready to enter first grade. I had hoped for a full-time position since we were running out of money. Then, I was hired as an editor. It seemed like a miracle. It was not an easy decision nor easy work. I was trained in preschool education, not in journalism, so there was much to learn. I was strengthened during those years—new friends, new work, new house, new church, and the children's adjustments.

I have discovered that joys and sorrows continue through life, one following the other. To be strengthened by sorrow and to feel bountiful joys have made life worth living.

"Clara" also faced an uncertain future as the shock of a death settled in.

I was told that my family cried all night when I married and went away to live. My husband and I went back home to visit our parents often. In about a year, we had a little daughter of our own. Within the next two years, we had another baby girl. My husband was a wonderful, loving husband and father to us.

A few years passed, and my husband contracted pneumonia—for the third time. No doctors knew what to do for it. I think he knew from the beginning that he would not recover again. He was put to bed and covered with blankets to make him perspire to get the "poison" out of his system. He was given chicken broth. A mustard plaster was put on his chest. We kept a roaring fire night and day for nine days. My husband died on December 30. He was 31 years old.

Our little baby daughter, two weeks old, also had pneumonia at the same time. She died December 29. I began to realize what a very heavy load was on my shoulders. This was just before the Great Depression in the 1930s. I knew I had to get to work and rear my little girls. The eldest was a first grader.

Work was very hard to get at that time. I knew I could not make a salary to support us and get someone to care for my children. I moved back in with my parents and walked a mile and a half into the city to find work. My parents had a cow, chickens, a garden, and canned foods. We did not have to buy much to eat.

I was very anxious for the children and me to get out on our own, which we finally did. Even then, I would sometimes lose my job and have to go back home for awhile until I could find work again.

When my children had dental work done or had to see a doctor, they had to go alone. I had to stay on the job. The doctor and dentist would make the price less than half for us. Bread cost five cents for two loaves. I gave ten percent of my very small income to the church. We walked to church a mile and a half on Sunday.

At night, I walked home from work, sewed, washed, and ironed the clothing we wore. God was our great provider in all things. We did not have a lot of sickness, but we had a lot of love. We were happy.

"Clara" knew real panic in dealing with so much responsibility at such a young age.

War and Death

Sadly, death sometimes ensues from the horrors of war. There is no way to prepare a family adequately for what could be ahead of them.

Elsie discovered that.

My friends thought that I had a premonition that Don, our son-in-law, would not return from the Persian Gulf War. I didn't. Since December 18, when he received his orders, we had begun to steel ourselves for his going. Christmas, 1990, was for us more an observance than a celebration. Our family withdrew into our own private world, trying to find comfort in each other, in firelight, and in quiet conversation.

The day after Christmas Don called to tell us that he was leaving for Saudi Arabia the next day. His F-15E was ready for the 17-hour flight. He also wanted to thank me for a letter I had written to him two weeks before. In it I had reminded him of some verses from Psalm 139 that had been consoling to me when I had sent my only son off to Vietnam:

"If I take the wings of the morning, and dwell in the uttermost parts of the sea; Even there shall thy hand lead me, and thy right hand shall hold me; even the night shall be light about me. Yea, the darkness hideth not from thee; but the night shineth as the day: the darkness and the light are both alike to thee."(Psalm 139:9-12)

Don's comment was, "I especially liked the part that says, 'The darkness and the light are both alike to God.' When you chose that, you didn't know that most of our work will be done at night. The F-15E can 'see' in the dark."

He knew I was worried, but he pulled no punches. Matter of factly, he declared, "We will be in the first air strike. Yes, it's very dangerous, but I've been well-trained; my pilot and I make a good team. Our plane is fantastic. You wouldn't believe what it can do!" I managed to remain composed, assuring him that we would be praying for him until he came safely home.

As the January 15 deadline for Hussein's compliance drew near and there were no signs of his meeting our terms, we realized that war was a terrible possibility. We felt a great urgency to be with our daughter and grandson when hostilities actually began. How providential it was that we were there with them on the evening of January 16 when CNN announced that the F-15E's had taken off for what was most likely the first air strike of the war. How merciful it was that we were there on the following evening when three cars wound slowly down the street and stopped in front of the house. From them emerged the Colonel, the Chaplain, and the doctor. We didn't have to ask why they were there. "Missing in action. . . ."

Thus began two months of indescribable anguish. Where was he? Was he dead? Injured? Was he in hiding? Hungry? Thirsty? Was he being tortured?

At first, we thought his plane had been lost over Baghdad. On a map of Iraq, we measured distances to the borders of the surrounding countries, hoping against hope that, if the plane was crippled, it could make it to one of those countries. Perhaps someone would hide him until the war was over. After the cease-fire, we learned that his plane was shot down over Basra.

Each time a list of casualties or prisoners of war was released and his name was not there, our hopes eroded. But, we held on until the last list. Then we turned off CNN. There was nothing to do but wait. . . .

On March 18, news came that the Iraqis were releasing his body. We buried him beside his grandfather, whom he adored. He was buried with full military honors. A "Missing Man" formation of F-15's flew low over the cemetery. One plane broke away and zoomed upward. We watched it shrink in the distance until it was no bigger than an eagle.

Now we are in slow and painful recovery. The out-pouring of concern, not only from friends, but even from people we didn't know who shared our grief and expressed their appreciation for his sacrifice, was overwhelming as well as comforting.

Prayer groups all over the country were praying for Don throughout the months he was missing, not knowing that he was probably killed instantly on that first day. We will never know.

I kept a journal day by day, knowing that later it would help me sort out my emotions. I find that writing about our experience is therapeutic.

For my own survival, I've tried to stay busy, doing something productive. When I sat idle, I began to sink in quicksand. So I took on a demanding assignment of a temporary nature that consumed my time and thoughts. My husband and I have tried to offer moral support to our daughter and her children, tried to help them begin the process of rebuilding their lives.

The other single most restorative activity was listening to beautiful music, especially sacred music. And singing! How could I sing at a time like this? I don't know. But for a little while, at least, I found I could find release from the prison of my sorrow and soar above it!

Someone has said, "Sorrow never leaves us where it finds us." We will never be the same again. We will never take the gift of life for granted, ever. We are much less sure of pat answers, much more aware of the necessity of taking *time* to savor life and people and experiences.

The Shock and Sorrow of Accidental Death

Unlike Don, Chuck's life did not seem to be in danger. Nevertheless, it ended early. Painfully, Cynthia tells of her life's greatest tragedy and of her grief and recovery.

Getting ready to go on a vacation is hectic. We were planning to drive all night. Our son, Chuck, would not be home until after a softball game that night. As I went out to buy our dinner, I saw lights still on at Joe's Sporting Goods. I knew that Chuck was still there. I went by to say goodbye to him. He kissed me, told me he loved me, and said, "Have a good time." I did not know then that that would be the last time I would ever see him alive on this earth.

October 12 we started home, anxious to get back. We were also anxious to get some rest before going to work the next day and anxious to see both our children. We stopped briefly in another city to see our daughter. Then I was ready to head for home.

When we got home, I thought Chuck was home because lights were on—but no Chuck. Blue jeans, shirts, and such (all dirty) were in the laundry room. I started a load of clothes. We unloaded the car, and I began putting things away.

Just then we saw headlights and thought Chuck had gotten home. It was about 11 P. M. It was our pastor and his wife, who told us that Chuck had been killed about 9:45 P. M. just a couple of blocks from home. The pastor said his car had flipped (it was actually his girlfriend's car) and he had been partially ejected through the sun-roof. My thoughts flew to his sister, who adored her big brother. My husband, Judd, and our pastor left town to go to the city where she lived, to break the news to her, and to bring her home. I finally went to bed about 5:00 A. M.

Loving friends brought food and flowers and were there to weep, laugh, and remember with us. Our daughter was working for a television station in the newsroom. All the news anchor-men and some of the women came to the funeral. I overheard someone ask, "Why is Channel 2 covering this funeral?"

Chuck had a host of friends—the entire hillside at the cemetery was covered with young people. We were at the cemetery about an hour. I found myself comforting his friends.

During the next week or two, I woke up in the night and heard his footsteps down the hall. We talked about Chuck many times, mentioning his name first, to make it more comfortable for others to do so.

I think Christmas is the most difficult time. Even now, after 11 years, as I begin to Christmas shop, before I can stop myself, I wonder, "What can I get for Chuck?" The first Christmas was very sad because he was killed in October. The Christmas before he was killed, he gave us a large photograph of himself, the one thing I really wanted. It still hangs in our living room.

Miss him? You bet I do. But, I'll be eternally grateful that he was killed instantly and did not have to live as a vegetable or a cripple. He was so athletic. We still meet people who tell us how much they thought of him. We also know that one day we will see him again.

In contrast to Chuck's death, how does a family recover from a violent murder in which they must deal with grief *and* forgiveness? Don and Evelyn Bicknese said that their family dealt with their pain by trying to make the world a safer place for all.

> Kent Bicknese, 22, was excited about his decision to take a break from college and work for his brother's outdoor advertising company for awhile. On February 8, 1983, only a few days after beginning his new job, Kent walked into a business to talk to the owner about a land lease. Moments later, Kent and two others were dead. Kent, an "innocent bystander," was killed by someone he had never seen before. Can you imagine this happening to you, your brother, your sister, parent, or a best friend?[1]

Transforming the Tragedy

Out of that tragedy grew the Kent Hollister Bicknese Foundation. Its purpose is to teach and encourage children, young people, and adults to improve their attitudes toward each other with compassion, kindness, forgiveness, unselfishness, self-respect, and respect for others. Two programs are sponsored by the Foundation. The Golden Rule Award is a program designed to encourage fourth, fifth, and sixth graders to live by the Golden Rule and to have goals to strive for. Mostly Manners is an etiquette course for children, teaching them self-discipline, consideration for others (the basis for crime prevention), and an understanding of why a good attitude is important in life.

The Foundation has taken positive steps in crime prevention by communicating with 3,000 schools annually and offering scholarships in middle and high schools for poster design winners in crime prevention. The winners' ideas are displayed on billboards nationwide. Other activities have included distributing crime-prevention literature and providing speaker panels for clubs and youth groups. Evelyn Bicknese says: "We need communities that offer safety . . . where kids can go out riding their bicycles again, play kick-the-can, and walk to the grocery store in safety."

A future plan of the Foundation includes providing educational assistance for nursery schools by showing ways to develop character through love and caring.

Jennifer Dean won First Place in the poster contest with the following design:

Design by Jennifer Dean, Hillwood High School, Nashville, TN

It says what Kent Hollister Bicknese would want to say. For that's how he lived his life—with love.

The Death of a Small Child

Sometimes life ends before one has had the chance to relish it. One of the most difficult things a family ever has to face and recover from has to be the death of an innocent child. The following story shows how even this tragedy can be transformed into something good.

The day my husband and I learned we were having twins was one of the greatest days I can remember. Our joy was immeasurable. To our surprise, however, when I was 19 weeks pregnant, the doctors told us that one of the babies was terminating itself. An ultrasound revealed that one of the babies, although about the same size as the other baby, was in a sack with virtually no amniotic fluid. The doctors explained that any procedure performed to correct the problem would result in premature labor and the death of both babies. After a long discussion with a specialist, we found that the one baby basically had no chance of survival and the other baby had only a 50 percent chance of survival—if, *and only if*, the one baby would terminate.

My only choice was to go home and stay in bed. Basically, I was to lie there, wait for one baby to die, and do the best I could to help the other one survive. My mother moved into our home to help with our two children, ages one and three.

We made simple arrangements with the undertaker back in my home town for our baby to be buried beside my father. I was obsessed with the fact that I wanted a name given to her before she was born. My husband and I finally reached an agreement to name her Angela, since she was to be our little angel.

Two weeks later during a regular appointment, my doctor was sure that he could still hear two heart beats. A week later, when I went in for an ultrasound, they were amazed to find Angela still alive and her condition improving. Once again I went home to bed. I was told to continue whatever I was doing, because it was working. I was then 25 weeks pregnant. Since Angela was continuing to progress (even if it was at a slow rate), she was to the point that if she started to terminate herself, the doctors could take both babies. Then, they would both have a chance to survive.

I entered the hospital. It was the beginning of what I thought would be two to four weeks. My stay ended up being 11 long weeks. None of this would have been possible if it had not been for a very supportive husband and mother, two loving little children, the support of a church in my home town, and the support of a church that I had not even joined.

Finally, at 35 weeks, the doctors decided that the babies were mature enough to be born. They performed a Caesarean. "Our little angel" was born with no sign of problems. Her sister, Andrea, was born with four heart problems, three of which corrected themselves within days. That left a congenital heart problem that would need to be corrected surgically. We were assured that it was a minor problem and that it would be best to wait until she was between six and 12 months of age before surgery. So we took our babies home.

On a regular basis, we went to the heart specialist. He ran tests on the girls. Since they were identical twins, the two of them could be compared. By the time the girls were nine months old, they were crawling. It became very obvious that Angela would take the lead while Andrea would have to lie down and rest periodically. At the next checkup, it was decided that maybe it would be best to go ahead with the surgery.

Once again, we were assured that this was a relatively simple surgery, that the worst that could happen would be that they could not successfully remove the obstruction that was restricting the blood flow. If that was the case, the next option would be open-heart surgery. The procedure they were going to perform was called a Baloon Angioplasty. The day came for surgery. The surgeon came over to us and told us that he would bring her back in two hours, not to worry, that all would go well.

Two long, miserable hours passed during which there was a lot of nervous chatter. Our pastor came to be with us. The head of cardiology came to the waiting room. He took my husband and me into another room with our pastor and told us that there were some major complications. The next 20 minutes were crucial for our daughter. Twenty minutes of pure hell is what we experienced; 20 minutes of praying to God to spare her life. The surgeon came into the room to tell us that she had not made it through the surgery. Our daughter had died. I was numb. I was mad. How could I go on without her?

I knew I wanted to hold her one last time. We went to another room and waited for our daughter to be brought to us. They laid her in my arms, and I looked down into her innocent, peaceful face. I remember that as I kissed her, I could feel how cold she was. I wanted to hold her forever, to make her warm—she was so cold. They took her from us, and we had to go home and leave her behind. We took her back to my home town to be buried beside my father.

I did not reach out to anyone over the next few months. Friends were still there for me, but I did not know how to hold on. Drinking was one of the ways that I could cope. The bad thing was that, when I sobered up, the pain was still there. One of my friends was there by my side, picking up the pieces.

I was not much of a mother or wife. I knew that I needed help. Finally, I reached out to a lady that I did not know that well. She got me the help I needed. She referred me to a counselor who has helped change my life. For one thing, I found out that it is okay to cry and be angry.

One Sunday, as I listened to our pastor's sermon entitled "Finding the Good," I thought, "What good could there be in the death of a child?" I searched my heart for the answer to that question. But, sometimes, answers are not there.

My husband and I had been searching for something to do as a memorial to Andrea. One day, the thought of a playground came to mind. We could build a playground in her memory so that many children could benefit. We made this dream come true. With the help of many others, we built a playground at our church. Many donations came in as memorials for other children who had died. Many people volunteered time to help build each piece that went into the playground. Not only was it good for us finally to find something that made our hearts feel good—it has also helped other parents with their grief.

I know that we have only started to rebuild our lives and that we have a long way to go. But, I also know that someday I will be able to hold my daughter in my arms again.

Marilee

Today, children come from miles away to play at the Andrea Kay Memorial Playground. Watching them, her family has found some healing from their grief.

Rebuilding lives is never easy after a death. "Lindy" wrote of her family's ordeal in her journal of the events.

Dublin, Ireland
June 1, 1984

I want to write down my thoughts about the past 10 days.

I was admitted to the hospital at 10 A. M. and Timothy and I were immediately put on a monitor. After about four hours, the doctors decided that Timothy was in too much distress to be delivered normally. The decision was made for a C-section. I was terribly excited. Our baby was going to be born.

Timothy Neal was born between 6:30 and 7 P. M., all three pounds and 11 ounces of him. He had lots of blond hair and blue eyes. We were so happy! We certainly were delighted with the day's accomplishment and even more excited that we had another son. We loved our Timmy.

My husband went home and I fell into a totally blissful sleep. I was awakened about 4 A. M. by the pediatrician. He told me that Timothy had had a rough go of it. He said his lungs weren't fully developed and he was probably more premature than we thought. He said that he had kept his lungs under a lot of pressure to keep them going and that might cause bleeding in the head. The doctor had done two brain scans and there was no bleeding. He said Timothy was going to be fine. When the doctor left, I went back to sleep immediately.

I was awakened about an hour later by another pediatrician. She told me that our baby had taken a turn for the worse and she didn't expect him to hold on for very long. She wanted to know if they could call anyone for me. I said, "My husband." I asked the doctor if there was any chance of Timothy making it. The doctor said "No, he won't pull through." It was so definite! I said very simply, "God, I know you have power over life and death. If you choose, he can live. I don't know what is best, but if it is your will, please spare his life."

My husband arrived just after seeing Timothy. Our baby was still alive. A few moments later, the doctor and a nurse came. The doctor leaned over my bed and speaking about six inches from my head, she said, "Your son has died." I nodded my head in understanding, and she left. My husband was beside me sitting in a chair. He laid his head at my side and wept, and I put my hand on his head.

Timothy was born on Monday. He died on Tuesday. His funeral was on Thursday.

I maintained my sanity and greeted our guests. At night I cried myself to sleep. We left the Emerald Isle on June 15, 1984. We never returned. Timothy remains in Ireland. His grave has no stone. I have vowed to return there someday, to lay a stone on his grave, and to lay his memory to rest.

Notes

[1]From the Kent Hollister Bicknese Foundation's 1991-1992 Public Awareness Campaign Theme Poster contest.

Chapter 11

A Long, Hot Summer in Georgia

I think I saw it in one of those "better home" magazines. It was a sublime scene with a fire in the fireplace and a round table with a "skirt" to the floor in front of the blazing fire, all beautifully set. "We'll do it that way," I said. I called our friends. Yes, they could come for dinner on Saturday night.

I already had a tablecloth. There was just one problem - the color didn't match the living room. I took myself to the drug store and bought several packages of "Cardinal Red" dye (it was actually a rose). I removed the fringe from the bottom of the tablecloth. The cloth consisted of a longer piece and a shorter piece which lay over that. When I pulled them out of the dye bath, they didn't quite match. So, I set about to correct that by giving one of them another bath. That meant going back to the store for more dye.

After the fringe-dyeing process, it was time to sew the fringe back on the bottom of the "skirt." I sat down at the sewing machine only to discover the machine didn't work. I would not be outdone. I sewed the fringe on by hand—no small task. I was determined to sew it on later by machine. As I got to the end, something was terribly wrong. At the place where the fringe was supposed to meet, it didn't. In the course of the dyeing process, it had shrunk.

"This is ridiculous," I thought. It was now Thursday. I went to the cloth store, bought a few more inches of ball fringe, went back to the drug store for another package of dye, and solved that problem. I sewed it into the missing bare space.

The night came for the party. Just before the guests arrived, we began our task of moving the round table from the breakfast room into the living room. Alas, the table wouldn't go through the door—a fact I hadn't even thought of! We carried it out the back door, around the house, and into the front door just before the guests arrived.

Skeptics won't believe that story, but it's true. There is, in each of us, a will that is undaunted. There is a determination to fight on, no matter how tall the obstacle. I have seen this over and over in people who have survived difficult illnesses and handicaps.

Fighting Cancer

"Jane's" determination is evident in the following account.

As I glanced in the mirror at 10 P. M. on a Thursday in June, 1979, while preparing to take my bath, I noticed a blue mark on the lower side of my left breast. My first thought was, "Hmmm, a blood vessel has burst." I put on my glasses and looked more closely, while my fingers probed the area. There was a lump. I knew instantly that I was in trouble. I stood there for a few minutes, then I got my bath, went to bed and prayed that God would be with me and help me to have the strength that I needed to go through what I anticipated would be happening.

I could hear my husband in his room snoring away. You see, he was as drunk as a skunk, which was his nightly ritual. I had no one to share with until I went to work the next morning and told my boss and my friend who was my assistant.

The next step was to call my surgeon's office and make an appointment. He saw me on Friday. When he felt the lump, he immediately announced that it must be removed the following Monday. When I told my internist, who is a personal friend, he cried. He had given me a physical in November, 1978, and he could not feel the lump at that time.

I knew when I was taken to surgery that I would come back without my breast. I was right. The report came back malignant.

I took chemotherapy for a year. The doctor explained the side effects—sickness, nausea, loss of hair, and so on. I was scheduled to take one treatment intravenously per month, then follow with pills for three weeks. I only had one week each month that I felt human. I elected to take my treatment on Friday so I could be sick on the weekend. After the treatment, I had to drive myself home. I felt so bad and so strange, I could hardly see the streets. My husband never offered to take me or to come and get me.

One day when I reached the back door, I could hear the television program "Dukes of Hazzard" playing rather loudly.

There sat my husband, already drunk, no help to me at all. I fell into bed and passed out. The next morning I had to start on the pills for three weeks.

Once, while I was taking chemo, I remember mentioning being sick and he said, "There is nothing wrong with you." He never once said,"I'm sorry you are having to go through this."

I continued to work every day because less than three months after I started treatment, my husband quit his job. He has not worked since. He was only 60 years old and could not apply for Social Security until he was 65. We needed my job to pay insurance and buy groceries.

Looking back after 12 years, it is hard to believe that I endured the pain and discomfort that I had. I managed to go to work every day. I never entertained the thought of dying.

My daughter, who lived in another state, was my support system. She came to visit often, and we talked by phone each week. I knew that I had a lot to live for.

I try to enourage cancer patients to have a happy outlook— don't be morbid. Stay busy, help other people.

In 1984, I had the other breast removed. This one was not malignant. I have had 12 years of life that I thank God for every day. Two years ago, my husband stopped drinking and two months ago, he quit smoking. These are truly two miracles that I have witnessed.

Edgar was shocked at the sudden discovery of his illness.

The last thing my wife had said to me before dropping me off at the airport several days earlier was: "Don't go to New Orleans and get sick and get in a hospital. I don't have time to fly down there." She found the time. It is a point of humor now.

I was in New Orleans on a teaching assignment when I became so ill that I decided to see a doctor at a local hospital emergency room. A glance at me obviously impressed him that I had more than a sinus infection. Following some tests, the doctor informed me that I was extremely ill and, in all probability, had leukemia. Tests on the following day verified it. It was August, 1989.

I remained in New Orleans until I was able to fly to my hometown to begin chemotherapy treatment. Following the first series of treatments, I was able to return home for eight weeks.

Major famiy decisions and actions were completed before I returned to the hospital for a second series of chemotherapy treatments, which was completed in January, 1990.

Life had led me, as it has others, into the valley of the shadow of death. But I was not alone in the valley. The initial shock, fear, exhaustion, worry, various irritations, long restless nights, and doubts have been resolved.

After two years, I recall vividly the hospital experiences and subsequent days of recuperation. I was able to return to my work in the late spring of 1990. One week following the birth of our grandaughter, I was holding her. What a joy!

Survival has been and continues to be a priority in my life. A loving and supporting family, friends, and fellow employees all combine to provide encouragement. It is a struggle. The occasional flashbacks, continuing nausea, and dizziness are reminders of my illness.

The hardest challenge comes not at the point of strength but at the point of helplessness and weakness. To "keep on keeping on" when you find yourself surrounded by immensities you cannot change—when there is nothing to do except hold on and try to endure—is the hardest challenge. When there is no occasion to soar and no place to run, then the promise of strength "to walk and not faint" becomes highly significant and appropriate.

Edgar has known depression, loneliness, and helplessness as a result of his disease. He says "I have known them all. But in it all, I have had hope. God has been faithful throughout the entire ordeal to provide comfort and to allow me to persevere."

A Life-Long Struggle

"Emily" was much younger when her devastating illness struck. "Polio" was the last thing her family wanted to hear.

The summer of 1954 was long and hot in Georgia. I was 18 months old. The feared disease Poliomyelitis was rampant and, in some cities, epidemic. Dr. Jonas Salk was working on the polio vaccine, but it was not until the following year that it was declared potent, effective, and safe. People were warned to keep their children away from public swimming pools, movies, and other crowded places. My parents followed all of these precautions and more. Nevertheless, I contracted the paralyzing disease.

After the acute symptoms of the illness were over, I began the long process of recovery. Hot packs were applied to my feet and legs. I had many long hours of physical therapy. I soon learned to walk with leg braces and crutches. By age two, I was home from the hospital with my family again.

Because I was so young, I gratefully have no memory of the actual illness. My parents tell me that I did not complain about my situation as a child. I was well aware that many people who contracted polio died. But, I survived.

In order for me to become as independent as possible, the doctors insisted that my parents encourage me to do everything for myself. They believed that my disability would not improve, but they also said that it would not get any worse. I believed my doctors, obeyed my parents, and never questioned my ability.

All of my surgeries, therapy, and other treatments were done at The Warm Springs Foundation, Warm Springs, Georgia. The Foundation, a major treatment facility for polio, was founded by President Franklin D. Roosevelt, who was also a polio survivor. He was my hero and role model.

I pushed myself to compensate. I graduated from high school, got married, went to college, and became an elementary school teacher. Teaching first graders, I was walking or standing constantly, rarely sitting down. The changes were subtle. I rarely used my crutches in the classroom. I only wore a brace on my left leg. Soon, though, I was again wearing a brace on my right leg and using my crutches more often.

During the next seven years, our two children were born. I found myself expending more and more energy doing daily activities. I began experiencing new pain and fatigue. My feet and legs hurt most of the time. I was trying to maintain an active lifestyle with a body that could not keep up.

I did not understand what was happening to my body. I certainly was not as active as I had been in the past. I felt all alone in this struggle. It never occurred to me that what was happening to me could be happening to others.

One day, while reading a newspaper, I noticed an article about polio survivors. The article reported that many of the 600,000 survivors were experiencing joint and muscle pain, fatigue, muscle weakness, and a loss of strength. These and other problems were similar to what they experienced when they first contracted the disease some 30 years before. The article went on to describe what is now known as "The Late Effects of Polio." For the first time, I realized that polio was not just locked into my past but commanding and changing my present as well.

I learned that a post-polio support group was beginning in the city in which I lived. I was very interested in meeting other people who had also survived the disease. I began attending the meetings. Most of those attending were much older than I. It seemed obvious to me that their physical disabilities were much worse than mine. I was in denial, mainly because I could not accept that the doctors who treated me during my childhood were wrong in saying that my disability would not get worse.

As I participated in the support group, I began to notice all the physical changes that had taken place in my body and lifestyle. I talked to other survivors and heard similar experiences. I read every article that I could find and went to the group meetings to learn to deal constructively with the emotional and physical changes. I once thought that I had recovered from polio, I now know that my life-long task of recovery is an ongoing process in which I must be actively involved.

By conscious decision, my activities are very different. I must rest often. I must shop at grocery stores that are smaller and more convenient. I plan my outings to make the best use of my energy. When I have a long distance to walk, I use a wheelchair. I know that if I use all my energy walking somewhere, then I am not able to enjoy myself once I arrive.

I try to help others deal with their disabilities in a positive way. Recovery is not easy. I must continue to learn all there is about my disability. It is a part of my life, but not *all* of my life. My understanding is greater and even easier because I realize that I am not alone in my struggle.

When Loved Ones Are Threatened

Bob and Libby had to face the serious illness and possible death of their child for other health reasons. The shock of discovering that a loved one has a severe or life-threatening illness can "undo us." With much feeling, Bob relates the events.

August 6 started like any other summer day in our household. My wife, who is a "stay-at-home" mom, was downstairs relaxing before the kids woke up and the onslaught of the day began. As the kids came downstairs, it struck her as unusual that Bennett would come over and lie down in her lap. He is typically, as are most two year-olds, a high energy child with two speeds—On/Off. This, coupled with the fact that a few months earlier he had had a febrile seizure, made my wife quite uneasy. Without overanalyzing the situation, she told all three kids to load up in the van. Off to the doctor they went.

After the usual examination revealed nothing, some poking and prodding revealed a lump in Bennett's abdomen. An x-ray showed nothing unusual. We were told to bring him back the next week before we left on our family vacation. As the excitement of the vacation neared and no signs of listlessness returned, we almost forgot to take him back for a re-exam. Thinking that she could take care of our daughter's school shots at the same time, Lib hauled them both back to the doctor's office. The doctor said she could still feel the mass in Bennett's abdomen. It was determined that a sonogram would be scheduled for the next morning.

When we returned the next morning, it was apparent that the doctors were anticipating something far more serious than we had ever considered. When the sonogram confirmed their suspicions, we were told to take no more than 30 minutes to pack some things and to take Bennett to Children's Mercy Hospital. It seemed as if the bad news continued to get worse. Three days later, our baby was recovering from four and a half hours of surgery to remove a neuroblastoma tumor from his uretor tube between his kidney and bladder. The bad news continued. Further testing revealed that the cancer had spread to his bone marrow. We were told to prepare for two years of chemotherapy and the possibility of a bone marrow transplant if he didn't respond to the chemotherapy.

A year later, after 62 days of hospitalization, six rounds of chemotherapy, numerous bone marrow draws, and countless medical procedures, Bennett is cancer-free. Other than his normal CAT scans and monthly exams, he is living a normal three-year-old life. Perhaps the greatest miracle in all of this is that we are stronger than we have ever been as a family as a result of Bennett's sickness. I cannot begin to tell of all the miracles that we saw and experienced or of the inexplicable "peace . . . which passes all understanding" (Phil 4:7, RSV).

Like all cancer survivors, "Louise" prayed it wouldn't happen to her again. How does one accept twice the news of a potentially fatal illness in herself and survive the discouragement? "Louise" did just that.

In the year 1969, I was the typical housewife and mother who enjoyed taking care of her husband and two children, ages 10 and 12. Since their births, I had gone for annual checkups with the doctor. In December of 1969, I had my routine checkup and was given a good report as usual.

In April, 1970, a small problem developed. I again saw my gynecologist. At that time, he found a cyst on my ovary that was not there four months earlier. We had planned a vacation, so he said, "Enjoy and come back in six weeks." At the end of that time, the doctor found that the cyst had grown to orange size and needed to be removed.

The morning after surgery, the doctor came in to tell me the bad news. The ovary was malignant. A complete hysterectomy was performed. In those days, cancer was not talked about very much. There seemed to be a real stigma attached to it. My first thoughts were, "I don't want anyone to know."

Twenty-five consecutive cobalt radiation treatments were given to me to kill the cancer cells. The radiation had severe side effects, some of which lasted for about six months. Lesser side effects continue to this day. That was 21 years ago. Little did I realize that cancer would strike again in a different location.

I was not ready for cancer to occur a second time. In the fall of 1990, I began to experience intermittent abdominal discomfort. I decided to see my doctor for a checkup. The tests proved to be negative. Our children and grandchildren came for Christmas. It was wonderful having them home. But, I was unable to eat or digest most of the good holiday food because of increasing abdominal pain. This prompted another visit to the doctor. After four days of tests, it was determined that I had an intestinal blockage that was malignant.

Having had cancer once before and survived it gave me the strength I needed to face surgery for the second time. Because the cancer had metastasized and was found in a second site, I accepted the fact that I would have a year of chemotherapy. Surgery was performed. My stay in the hospital lasted 19 days.

A month later, the chemotherapy treatments were started and given intravenously once a week in the doctor's office. Because of the destructive effect of the weekly chemo treatments, the veins in my hands collapsed. A port-a-catheter was implanted in my chest to allow the medicine to be continued.

Surgery was a year ago. The chemo is finished, and the port-a-catheter has been surgically removed. I have very positive feelings about the future. The support and prayers of family, friends, and people I have never met have played a very important role in my recovery. I want to live life to the fullest!

"Louise"

The crisis came on a Tuesday. Quick medical action, long therapy, and determination helped "Margaret" to survive and recover.

For the life of me, I cannot remember March 6, 1990, or anything that happened during the five weeks that followed. I arose at my usual hour (5:30 A. M.) to prepare for my job as principal of a nearby junior high school. I complained of the "worst headache I've ever had in my life," while my husband continued trying to extend his sleep. He was awake enough, however, to be aware that I was crawling back into bed, something I had never done during my 30 plus years of working in the public schools. He promptly rolled over and dialed 911.

The paramedics arrived within a few minutes and promptly diagnosed my problem as a cerebral hemorrhage. They alerted the hospital that I would soon arrive. At the hospital, the doctor, a respected neurosurgeon, was waiting for me. Numerous tests and examinations revealed that I was suffering from a subarachnoid hemorrhage and that the amount of blood in the brain was so extensive that it was impossible to determine the source of the bleeding. He scheduled a second angiogram and surgery for the next day surgery.

Meanwhile, he informed my family that I was near death *and that they should not expect me to live.* When the angiogram was repeated the next day, the same problem existed: too much blood to see the source. I had 15 or more seizures during the night. Death was imminent. Then, he recommended to my family a course of treatment that we had never heard of. I was placed in a chemically-induced coma, while the functioning of my body was given over to machines. For three weeks, I lay in a coma.

Family members kept a constant vigil in the waiting room. They planned my funeral. Three weeks later, when it became necessary to reduce my medication, remove the machines, and bring me out of the coma, my family did not expect me to survive. Instead, I survived but was totally unresponsive. I was transferred to another hospital.

Sometime around April 8 or 9, I remember awakening during the night and wondering where I was. I had been there since April 2. I began to emerge from my cocoon. Very fine therapists directed my recovery. I left the hospital six weeks later, walking on my own power, able to handle most of the ordinary tasks of daily living.

Physical therapy was demanding and exhausting. Cognitive therapy helped me unscramble the short circuits in my brain and restore normal functioning. I continued with outpatient therapy for six weeks after my return home on Mother's Day, 1990.

The doctor says that I am a miracle. Most remarkable, he says, is that I came out of the experience with no serious disabilities, for which I give gratitude to God.

Ongoing Hardships

Champions of courage are those who live with ongoing handicaps. One such as "David's" must be dealt with day by day and with great patience.

"David" is blind. "Sarah" is sighted. "If the issues of a blind/sighted marriage aren't taken care of before the marriage, the couple may find themselves in an emotional dilemma, not realizing what was involved." says "David." "It is essential that some of these issues are brought into the forefront or there may be a lot of unstated resentment at a later date."
"David" talks about some of the problem areas.

One of the biggest problems for a blind person is transportation. Even at best, bus service can be terrible. Although a sighted person is willing to help, he or she may become resentful of having to carry the full load of transportation. "Make as many true sighted friends as possible," "David" advises, "You may need them, as in the case when 'Sarah' broke her ankle. I asked for assistance for two and a half months."

For a blind person, everything has its place. Experience has shown that not keeping utensils and such in an organized manner can result in chaos. A sighted person can scan a drawer; a blind person cannot. This can cause problems.

Keeping finances in order is also a problem. This leaves most of the financial responsibility of bookkeeping up to the sighted spouse. It is difficult for a blind person to write checks. The bank must oftentimes ask, "Is this his signature?"

A "must" in a blind/sighted relationship is a good sense of humor. The ability of both partners to laugh at each other's mistakes, as well as their own, can be an asset.

A lot of responsibility is given to the sighted person regarding yard work. This is in addition to maintaining the house's plumbing, heating, and air conditioning. This is one reason many totally blind persons choose to live in an apartment. They may not have children or pets, since the rules of many apartments do not allow either.

Despite the preceding facts, however, a blind/sighted marriage has as much chance of surviving as a "normal" relationship.

His wife, "Sarah," says:

Being married to a blind person is a challenge, but it does give you a sense of well-being, of contentment. At least, it does for me. There are times I don't think I can make it. But with my hubby's help, his strength, his patience, and his love, things always seem to work out okay. A lot of the responsibility *does* fall on the sighted person's shoulders. But, whatever happens, don't give up, she advises. Being married to a blind person has its rewards. And you won't discover those if you don't stick around. Believe me, it's worth it!

In a lighter vein, Lucy's story is an example of determination.

When I was growing up, my parents told me never to faint in church. One day I felt as if I might. But I thought about it, and I decided not to.

So there you have it! The reason all of the above have been able to survive is their determination, will-power, and continuing help from those who love them.

Chapter 12

Fury and Firepower

Crack houses

Prostitution

Homicides

Lack of gainful employment

Drive-by shootings

What image does that collection of words and phrases bring to mind? It could be an apt description of a gang neighborhood, where violence is widespread.

We know the "whys" behind the violence:

- High unemployment (25 percent in some black city neighborhoods)

- Weapons in the hands of teenagers with no sense of mortality

- Family neglect

- Illegal drugs

- Early variety and frequency of anti-social behavior in children

- School failure

- Lack of job skills or training

- Lack of constructive activities to make use of free time

The Power and Threat of Gangs

How could any child grow up in that kind of environment and not be adversely affected? Gang neighborhoods are often described as "24-sevens," meaning the drug trafficking there goes on 24 hours a day, seven days a week. Shootings occur any time of the day or night. Four or five crack houses may crowd one block. Often elementary school dropouts work as drug runners. They deliver crack on their bicycles with crack hidden in the handlebars. Much of the money that used to go for food now goes for crack cocaine. "It's like a siege," said one resident of a gang neighborhood. Hot weather is an especially bad time because more people tend to spend more time outdoors.

What is the appeal of gangs to youth? Teens join gangs for protection or to find structure lacking in homes without fathers. Some join out of boredom. Some adolescents technically are not in a real gang; they just call themselves a gang. A short time in jail may reform them. Or, they get out because of the violence they see. They don't want to be the next victim. Others may be members of a bona fide gang.

"Hitman"

"Hitman" saw the dangers and separated himself from gang activity. He agreed to be interviewed. I met a handsome black man with a beautiful smile.

> Q: What led you into a gang lifestyle?
> A: For some youth it is lack of love at home or poverty. The gang assures the selling of drugs for money, a feeling of importance and self-respect, and unity of brothers. I had too much love at home. I wanted to experience things for myself—to learn about life on the streets by being part of a group.
> Q: Do you think that most youth feel a need to rebel at some time, to be independent from their parents?
> A: Definitely. That's a part of it.
> Q: What is your definition of a gang?

A: A group of several individuals who are out to kill, steal and destroy.

Q: What was the name of your gang?

A: I ended up forming my own. It was called the Southside Posse. It started with six people and ended up with 300. It is now called the Southside Crips. It started as a nice group that helped senior citizens. We had fundraising parties to buy paint so we could paint the homes of senior citizens free. When the parties stopped and we had no way of earning money, the group started making money in other ways. We started going our separate ways and getting into trouble.

We began with sticks and bats. As I was getting out to get married, we were beginning to use revolvers, shotguns, Uzi's, AK-47's and semi-automatic weapons. Today, gang members carry fully-automatic and semi-automatic weapons. They use "street sweepers" that blow up cars and everything else. They are carrying more weapons than an army.

Q: What insignia identified your group?

A: Hands crossed at the wrists and the words "Posse Up." Gang members use spray paint to mark a "set" (their turf, territory) by putting their insignia on the walls. If you go back later and it isn't erased, your gang can take it as your own turf. This is how the territories are identified. Through hand signals, as well as colors, gang members show their gang and the turf they are claiming. All of the clothing they wear must be the same color that the turf calls for—from shoe strings to hat. In California, the color of the "rag" they wear indicates what city of Crips and Bloods they belong to. Long Beach Crips, for instance, wear aqua-colored "rags."

Q: Did you witness violent crimes done by the gangs, such as armed robbery or murder?

A: Yes.

Q: Did all of you carry guns?

A: Only certain ones. The "henchmen," carried guns as a means of protecting the drug sales.

Q: Were you involved with drugs yourself?

A: Yes, mostly alcohol, but I tried a little of everything.

Q: Are most gang members "doing drugs?"

A: Yes, they both use and sell drugs. They use because of the pressures. They use mostly heroin because they feel the drug makes them tougher. They can shoot someone and feel no pain about doing it. Gangs buy drugs from each other.

Q: How long were you a member of the Southside Posse?

A: I began at the age of 16 in high school, and was a member for eight years. My age is 25 now. I am known as an "original gangster," which means that, if you are still alive after you turn 25, you can go on any gang's turf and be respected. You can only be an "original gangster" if you survive to the age of 25.

Q: How would they know if you are 25?

A: They keep up with it to the year and day.

Q: What should we, as ordinary citizens, fear from groups like the Crips and Bloods?

A: Mass destruction. We cannot stop it anymore than we can stop drugs, though we can slow it down. The more that gang/drug activity is publicized, the more it escalates. Gangs love publicity. They look for people to kill. It swells the homicide statistics. They would like to make our city the "home of the body bags." I didn't want to be another statistic. That's why I got out.

Q: Were you afraid when you tried to remove yourself from the group?

A: The only way you can leave a gang is on a positive level—to go out and do good. You can't do something positive and then go back to a gang, they will not accept you. You leave with love to do better and then you don't go back. The gang wants you to better yourself. The rules are: don't forsake or mistreat your family. When you do make it, don't ever forget who you came from. The gang paid for me (with drug money) to attend two years of business college, they wanted me to succeed. I made straight A's. They respected me for trying to succeed, but they needed my help with the different types of things in our group.

Q: Do you think education is important?

A: Very important

Q: It has been said that black mothers "bird dog" their sons through the difficult years in order to keep them alive? Do you agree with that?

A: No, what they do is assure their sons that they are men. Then, they send them out to the world to struggle and overcome it. They do the same with daughters. The sons and daughters are already seen as "low potential" by society with many slashes against them. They are taught to do good to a society that does not see them as valuable.

Q: What can we do for young children to keep them out of gangs and out of trouble when they get older?

A: We must get them before they get started into gangs. Keep them in church, take up time with them, answer their questions. Don't let them have to get out on the street. We should watch the news, learn all we can about street gangs, pray, fast, treat people as humans, no racism. We are all looking for love.

Q: Describe your family when you were growing up.

A: I have a beautiful family. They were church go-ers. My mom was saved, and I was saved. I now have a wife and three children and another on the way. (I saw tears in Hitman's eyes.)

Q: Why are you back in jail?

A: I was sent back for a crime I didn't commit that someone attributed to me. What hurt me the most was that my good name was tarnished. The fellow who did the shooting said he did it, but no one would believe him. I couldn't disprove the charges against me because of my past. I am no longer charged, and I will soon be free. I have never before been convicted or paroled or locked up for more than four days.

Q: What makes you happiest?

A: I'm happy because I found God again. One day I was sitting in jail and thinking, puzzled. "God allowed this to happen for a reason. I wasn't going to church. Once I seek God again, everything else will fall into place."

Q: When you get out of jail, will you go back to church?

A: Most definitely.

(Note: "Hitman" is the founder of "The Christian Coalition, In God We Trust," an organization that aids prisoners, their families, and other needy persons.)

"#2787322"

Like "Hitman," "Lamar" discovered that nothing good comes from being involved in gang activity.

"Tough as steel, but with a change of heart." That's how a police sergeant describes "Lamar," who lives on the campus of a correctional facility. Nine hundred inmates between the ages of 17 and 25 are incarcerated there. He describes a typical day.

I'm still in the roughest house on the hill because of my temper. I get up at 3:00 A. M. and work until 7:35 A. M. in food services. Then I go back to the dorm from 7:35 A. M. until 11:00 A. M. Lunch is at noon. From 1:00–4:00 P. M., I go to school (I quit school in the tenth grade. Eventually I will get a high school diploma, if I work at it.) Then, they count us back into the dorm. Supper is about 5:00 P. M. From 4:00 to 10:30 P. M., I can go to the gym to play basketball. I don't go much, though, because there are fights there. I can watch a movie, play cards, or talk on the phone. We have lights out at 10:30.

"Lamar's" problems began when he was seven years old. He saw his mother shot and killed. It filled him with thoughts of "I don't care anymore, I have nothing to live for." Then, his grandmother took over the care of him. She was the positive person in his life. Within two months, she was dead. Then, he was given over to the care of an uncle who beat him. Once he suffered a cut on the head after being hit in the head with a skillet. Because of the beatings, he was placed in a foster home at about the age of 13. After that, his family split up. He has two brothers and two sisters. He began to wish revenge on those who had done wrong to him.

Eventually "Lamar" became involved with a gang—the Beam Street Posse. Many of his friends were a negative influence. He drank alcohol but was not an alcoholic. He was arrested for the illegal sale of cocaine and for probation violation. He was a cocaine dealer but not a user. He was passing when he quit school. His girlfriend tried to keep him in school. He says, "She loved me for me. But the lure of money was too great. It was the fast money, jewels, cars, girls, and gold teeth that I liked too much. I was wearing $150.00 tennis shoes and $80.00 jackets. I'd give all that back now to have my freedom."

"Gangs can operate anywhere," he says, "but they set up shop in the ghetto because there the income is low and they can easily persuade the people that selling drugs will get them whatever they want."

He further explains that one can tell a gang member by the way he dresses, the way he talks, and the words he uses. If someone is wearing all blue in Blood territory, it could mean his life.

He adds, "And yes, they trip off blue socks as well as blue jackets and pants."

A gang member often wears a "rag" signifying the gang he belongs to. He might wear it on his head or arm, or he might possibly tie it around the gun in a drive-by shooting so the enemy will know who is shooting at them.

"The top man in a gang is called a leader," he says. "You get to be the leader by having the jewelry, money, drugs, and firepower (guns). Everyone considers him the toughest one of the bunch, and everyone does what he says."

"Lamar" is nineteen. His sentence is 10 years. He goes before the parole board in December, 1993. At that time, he will probably get a two-year outdate. He is looking at three more years of incarceration. He is the father of two.

> "You hurt more than yourself when you get locked up—your kids, your family. Your children spend years without their father," he says. "When I leave here, I'll be a changed person in many ways. I would say that I'm now recognizing and realizing my mistakes and rehabilitating my life. If I can steer one or two people to live right, I will have accomplished something."
>
> "Many of the fellows here will go back to their old lifestyle once they're out, mostly because of the fast money. The system only teaches guys to be slicker. Some of them have been locked up so long, they can't make a decision for themselves. They get $7.50 a month, three meals a day, and clothes to wear. They have someone else to make their decisions for them."
>
> "We have to learn to think about the mistakes we've made and learn from them. We don't have all the answers."

"Lamar" says he's happy to still be alive. He was shot five times, once by the Crips gang. He said:

> Out there some people are six feet deep and I'm still alive. Here there are no guns or knives. Find someone positive in your life and set goals for yourself. Nothing good comes from running with a gang. It's a quick trip to the graveyard or life in prison, and a lot of unnecessary trouble.

Gang members see themselves as loyal to each other and against the rest of the world. Gangs give young men a sense of belonging and status in neighborhoods where there is little stability. Members of the well-known Crips and Bloods gangs go in and out of our major cities. Their travels have taken them to as many as 32 states or more. They are businessmen who don't care who they hurt.

"Denton"

Peter Hernon has given the following account of his research among street gangs.

"Denton" chronicles the activities of gangs in order to find solutions to the problem. He was eight years old when a rapist grabbed his mother from the shadows as she walked to a bus stop. Fortunately, she was wearing her "old faithful" girdle and carrying a straight razor. Her attacker was unable to rip off the tight girdle, and, in the struggle, she pulled out her razor and slashed him across the throat. Her assailant ran off, trailing blood down the street.

Now age 35, and with a bachelor's degree in Justice Administration, "Denton's" job is to find gang members as part of a nationally funded project. Crips, Bloods, and other gang members call him "Street Daddy."

In 1982, he was riddled with gunfire as he sat in a car at a drive-in bank. The attack was in revenge for court testimony he had given in another shooting. The last bullet shattered his spine at belt level, paralyzing him from the waist down.

Now, armed with a cellular telephone, a stack of business cards, and a talent for rapping with strangers, he drives the worst streets of the city, pulling to the curb and climbing out of his wheelchair. He has brought many gang members in for interviews. Names are not taken; anonymity is guaranteed. The information is compiled to draw conclusions about how to deal with the gang problem.

"Denton" says, "The most shocking thing I've seen is the almost inhuman feeling about maiming and killing. The uncaring coldness you see in the faces of these kids, it stays with you." "Denton" reads the gang grafitti. "When you see the grafitti, the gang's are very close." One block might be claimed by one gang, the next by another. "It goes block by block," he says. "They're on top of one another. It's a turf thing with these gangs, and they're so close together, the violence can get out of hand." One can be in serious trouble if he is one block off his turf. Wanna-be's (want-to-be-gang members) are often more violent than the real thing.

One of his memories of lying in the hospital after the shooting that paralyzed him was the visit from a friend. He says:

> He was telling me about prayer and forgiveness and how I had to go on. I remember that it stormed that day. And, after he left, that storm rinsed my bitterness away. It just washed it away. And I was ready to get on with this new life and make the best of it.[1]

A survivor and hero in the gang wars is Joe Clark. Margo Webb tells his story.

> Joe . . . became principal of one of the worst high schools in America: East Side High in Paterson, New Jersey. When Clark arrived he found the school covered with grafitti. Teachers were scared of their students. Gangs roved the school at will, beating up students and openly selling drugs. Of course, nobody could study or learn, and the school had a terrible rating on achievement tests.
>
> Clark decided to take some risks. First he got the school board to provide the school with a good security force of twelve strong men. Next he got the names of all the drug dealers, gang members, and goof-offs—and he expelled them from school permanently.
>
> The parents of the expelled students were angry, but Clark ignored them. "I have to look out for the good students, not the bad ones," he said. His bosses backed him up.
>
> Clark put chains and padlocks on the school doors to keep the drug dealers and gang members out. He made up a dress code so the students would look neat. Nobody could wear gang colors. He made everyone learn the school song so they would have pride in their school.
>
> Joe Clark is a hero to some people, a villain to others. But one thing is sure: He showed what a principal and a school board can do if they really want to.
>
> National magazines put Clark on their covers, and television shows begged him for interviews. Somebody even made a movie about his successes at East Side High. The movie was called *Lean on Me.*[2]

The problem of a negative lifestyle may not be gang-related but merely associated with a life of crime. Some of those incarcerated say their problems began in not-so-stable families. Many also did not have positive role models, two-parent homes, or people going to work regularly in their neighborhoods. Their stories of survival and recovery are joyful ones.

Only the Strong Survive

"Jamie" entered prison the first time in 1982 for possession of a controlled substance and first degree robbery and burglary. He has been sent to county jail numerous times. He presently serves time for stealing goods in excess of $150.00. His age is 31. He came to his present facility only for a drug treatment program of 120 days. His sentence, however, is four years and he has another case pending.

His troubled life began when he was five years old. His dad was an alcoholic. That brought problems with his mother. The court system took away all eight children from the parents and the children were split up and placed in foster homes. The loss of a family had a very negative effect on "Jamie." The family was partially reunited after one and a half years, when his father gave up alcohol.

"Jamie's" drug problems began at age eleven, when he started sniffing lighter fluid. His usage progressed to marijuana, alcohol, acid, barbiturates, and heroin. His friends were a negative influence. He felt more accepted in a negative group than a positive one. The emotions of resentment toward his father and mother and self pity drove him to his negative lifestyle. "I quit school in the sixth grade," he says. "I never went to high school. I got my Grade Equivalency Diploma (GED) at age 23. It is the first thing I ever accomplished."

After his first release from prison, he stayed sober for three years. Then came problems with his wife. He went back to drugs. He stole to support his heroin habit, which was $300.00 a day. His mother died in 1989, an event which also took its toll on him. Only in prison has he realized that alcohol has made him do things he didn't even know he was doing. He had blackouts and doesn't even remember some of his crimes.

"Jamie" has survived prison by putting on a tough face—in prison only the strong survive. "I'm beginning to recover," he says. "Trying hard not to go back to the old lifestyle. Doing wrong is easy. When you try to live a normal life in society, that's hard."

After release, he hopes to live with his father, get a job, and work a recovery program. "A family that sticks by you is very important in recovery," he says. There will be problems awaiting him—staying sober and regaining the trust of his family.

His advice to youth who have never been incarcerated: "Look for strong family ties. Don't do drugs. It takes willpower and guts to make a good life for yourself. Life's a hard road, and it takes a lot of work, but you can get through it. Stick to a goal. Get an education. My father taught me morals, manners, and values," he said. "I just didn't take heed."

"My happiest times are when I am with my family," he says. "One dream I always had when my father and mother split up was to be together again as a family with the parents and all eight children. That never happened."

(Note: "Jamie's" father is a recovering alcoholic who works voluntarily with youth in drug treatment programs.)

Assault, Second Degree

Rikki is well-educated but the abuse of drugs led him into a poor lifestyle and subsequent confinement.

Q: What act or crimes led you to prison?
A: Assault, second degree.
Q: What is your age now and how long have you been here?
A: Age 36; two months
Q: How old were you when your troubled life began . . . the kind of life that sent you here to prison?
A: My father was an alcoholic. I was always around agressive behavior and violence. My problems began at age eight. It was an emotional type of confusion that later at age 16 led to alcohol and marijuana. I had no legal problems then, just social problems. I wrecked a car under the influence of alcohol. All of this leads to a certain lifestyle. This behavior is centered around anti-social things.
Q: Were you involved with other drugs?
A: Yes
Q: Which ones?

A: In college I used LSD, mescaline, speed, and cocaine. I graduated from college. I had a track scholarship. Grade-wise I did okay, but I would have done better without drugs. My drug of choice was cocaine.

Q: Would you say that you are now recovering from that kind of lifestyle?

A: I'm hopeful that I am recovering. I know that if I get involved with it again, it will lead me back to incarceration. I know that my behavior has affected a lot of people.

Q: Do you have plans for the future when you are released?

A: Yes, to teach school, since my degree is in that; to make amends to people, to get married and raise a family. All of this is dependent on whether or not I maintain sobriety.

Q: Will you be strong enough to resist the challenges on the outside?

A: I hope so. Doing drugs again could lead to everything wrong in my life. I must find other positive things to do. There will probably be some depression and a feeling of instability. I have always been able to get a job. Holding one could be a problem. If I become separated again from God, this will lead to problems.

Q: How have you survived prison? What gave you hope each day?

A: Technically, this is not a real prison situation. We are in protective custody here. There are 50 of us who are here for a 120-day drug treatment program. We are sent here because our cases are related to drugs. But on the prison grounds, there are approximately 2,000 inmates.

Q: Tell me about your family.

A: I came from a dysfunctional family. My father is an alcoholic. My parents were divorced during the first year of my life. He has always kept in touch with me. He has a heart of gold, but he is an alcoholic in denial. My mother is a codependent in denial. She bailed me out of a lot of things. I have one sister who is very upstanding—no drug problems. I have two older brothers. My middle brother is an alcoholic with two years of sobriety.

Q: What about the neighborhood you were in growing up. Were the people there a negative influence?

A: My friends were a lot like me. We were into sports, and we didn't like girls. I had a very nice set of friends.

Q: Has there been anything positive for you about your incarceration here?

A: Yes, I accepted Jesus into my life. A man named Charles Lee, who is a recovering alcoholic, conducts spiritual classes here. I attend the class. My mother was a church-goer, but I didn't go much. I was desperate when I accepted Jesus. I had been doing things *my way*, and it wasn't working out. I really feel like this has changed my life.

Q: What makes you happiest?

A: When I can honestly look at myself in the mirror and feel that it is not too late—there is always hope. I'm on the right road.

The Trouble Starts Early

If ever there was a man who walked in darkness who now walks in the light, it is "Stony." He also agreed to an interview. We met in a tiny room. I won't forget him or his story.

Q: Tell me about your past, especially your experiences with anti-social behavior.

A: I was nine years old when I drank my first beer. My uncle bought me a six-pack for my birthday. Another one of my uncles hung out with older guys. When they went upstairs to the vacant top floor of our four-family flat, I went with them and got very drunk. I was ten years old then. My uncle told me not to mess with the beer, but I got into it anyway. I started drinking a lot when I was 15.

Q: What is your sentence here?

A: I have a life sentence.

Q: What crime did you commit that was serious enough to warrant a life sentence?

A: I was convicted of beating to death an 86-year-old man who was a neighbor about four or five houses down from my grandmother's house. I went in to get money for alcohol. I got paranoid. I stayed in the front room only. The man's wife said, "Is it money you want?" I didn't answer her. "I'll go get it," she said. She brought it to me. It was $35.00. I think I scared her. I didn't go in for the purpose of hurting anyone. I went in because I was "high" on alcohol. I never broke into anyone's house. I was 26 years old when it happened. When I left the house, the man and his wife were both alive. The doctor's report said he had only one bruise on him and that he died from pneumonia.

Q: How old are you now?

A: Thirty-two

Q: Is there a chance you'll ever be released?

A: I will have a parole hearing in 1999. I can't have a hearing before then.

Q: When you were growing up, did your friends influence the kind of life that you have now?

A: My friends looked up to me because I was the oldest in a group of four to five people. They didn't lead me into anything bad. Our crowd wasn't easily influenced. My closest friend, however, later got into crack cocaine. He died when he ran into a tree at 100 miles per hour.

Q: What was your experience with alcohol after you started drinking a lot at age 15?

A: I never used hard drugs, but I was hooked on alcohol. I sometimes drank four or five six-packs at a time. I got up every day at 5:00 A. M. and went to work. Most of my problems were on the weekend. I never thought I had a problem. I had fights with my wife. She was trying to tell me, "Either quit drinking or slow down with it." The desire for alcohol was very strong. I would give all my money to my wife except $15.00 to $20.00 out of a paycheck, which I kept back to buy drinks. I never had any treatment for the problem.

Q: Were you on good terms with your parents?

A: I never knew my real father. My stepfather was a school-teacher and worked at other jobs at night. We never went hungry and we had everything we needed. My parents didn't drink alcohol or fight or get violent and hurt each other. My parents warned me that I would end up dead or in prison. I didn't think they knew what they were talking about. Now, I believe it. When you first get here and you have nothing in your hand from your past life, you lay down on your bed and cry. You're somewhere you don't want to be—with people who don't care anything about you. The guys here try to trick you out of everything they can.

My lock-up changed my parents' lives. They never went to church before. Now they do.

Q: You're a changed person too. How did that happen?

A: I didn't find the Lord until I went to jail for the crime that sent me here. One of the inmates gave me a Bible. "Take this Bible to your cell and read it," he said. But I could barely read. Ever so often, I would have to yell over to another cell and ask, "What is g-r-a-c-e? or f-a-i-t-h?" Someone would tell me. When I started reading it, something inside me was getting fed and it felt good. I got down on my knees in city jail, cried, and asked God to forgive me. It was April 6, 1986. I'll never forget that day. Then, a police lieutenant who was assigned to my case started writing me letters about the Lord. He didn't sign his name, but I knew who he was. After I got into prison, he continued to write letters to me. Then, he started putting his name and address on them. I brought God into prison with me.

I ask the Lord to watch over me day by day. Once I go out of my cell, it's a blessing to get back in without harm.

Q: It's been said that, once someone gets out and starts to face the problems on the outside, he may actually wish to be back in again because he feels "safe" here. Do you think that's true?

A: Yes, some inmates have been here 17 to 19 years and don't even want to go home. Some say this *is* their home.

Q: Why, in your opinion, do some inmates go back to a life serious of crime after prison?

A: Some guys don't try to rehabilitate themselves in here. Their whole conversation is trash and threats. Some don't care about themselves at all. Some of their families are glad they're locked up. Some don't receive any mail or any money from their families. If a man rehabilitates himself in here, he has a good chance of not coming back. My family has been support to me. I have a mom and dad and four sisters. I talk to them on the phone, and they visit me in the summer.

Q: What makes you happy?

A: When I see my family or talk to them on the phone. That gets me through another six to seven months in here, just knowing someone cares. There are people in here no one cares about, and they can't handle the depression.

Stony's story is typical of those whose problems in life began early. In the larger cities, a large percentage of the murders are committed by young (ages 17 to 25) black males. They often kill one another, and it is not uncommon for these violent acts to be connected with other crimes (such as robbery and drug deals) or alleged gang activity. Inner-city youth especially need someone to look up to and someone to spend time with them in order to provide direction and to help steer them toward self-respect. Community crime prevention is so much easier than the recovery of lives from bad choices and negative lifestyles.

In the final chapter, you will see how one community is dealing with crime prevention and surviving the drug war. I hope that it will serve as a model for your community.

Notes

[1]Peter Hernon, "Scholar Seeks Out Answers on Tough Streets," *St. Louis Post Dispatch*, 22 September 1991.

[2]Margo Webb, *Coping With Street Gangs* New York: Rosen Publishing Group, 1990) 131. Used with permission.

Chapter 13

A Community Survives (and Fights Back)

On a fall evening in 1983, 400 parents in the Kirkwood community on the west side of St. Louis, Missouri, went to one of their local high schools to view the video *The Chemical People,* a program promoted by Nancy Reagan as a part of her nationwide campaign against drug abuse.

The parents were so shocked at what they saw that they began to organize themselves to fight the drug problem. Kirkwood High School Principal, Franklin McCallie, said:

> When I came to the school in 1979, we were apprehending students with marijuana. Within the next couple of years, a significant amount of marijuana was being used and sold on campus. In fact, just before I came, the school had hired a college student to be in the school's smoking area because there was so much drug usage. The school was aware of the problem.
>
> The school's parents also knew there was a problem because we shared the information with them. However, at that time, there was no interaction between parents, the community, and the schools in the area of drug prevention. *The Chemical People* spawned a combined effort among the three.

Citizens in the newly-formed task force named their group PACK (Parents Actively Concerned, Kirkwood). With the help of parents such as Peggy Adams and Jean Likes, an all-out effort was launched against the problems of youth. The group agreed that, while the abuse of chemicals was of primary concern, there were other equally devastating problems affecting the youth. These problems included eating disorders, depression, suicide, and unwanted pregnancies. Meeting once a month, the members set the following goals.

• To be a citizen's support group for the school district and community

• To develop drug-free activities for youth

• To educate parents, teachers and students about the harmful effects of drugs

• To be a resource for information about drug and alcohol abuse

As a result of the group's efforts, the School Board appointed a committee to explore and develop a health curriculum for the school district. It was also decided to introduce a pilot program at the 5th grade level. The program chosen was Project Aware, sponsored by the Rotary Clubs of America. The behavior-modification module was an eleven-week program dealing with peer pressure, problem-solving techniques, and inter-personal relationships.

One PACK member, Ernie Baker, developed a high-school program called the Wilderness Club. Students signed up for outdoor activities including camping, hiking, and climbing. The outings sometimes included parents and family groups.

PACK also encouraged local restaurants, bars, liquor stores, and grocery stores to check I.D.'s. The group sponsored workshops for parents and teens and voted to send two high school students to the Missouri Teen Institute (a training seminar on substance abuse and prevention programs.)

PACK urged parents:

• To support an alternate activity when their children choose not to attend an unchaperoned party

• To communicate a clear position of "no drug use" to their children, and to state the consequences of drug abuse

• To withold permission for parties in hotel rooms

- To call the parents of any youth using drugs or appearing under the influence, and also to call the local law-enforcement agency

- To discourage youth from driving under the influence by teaching them the legal consequences of drinking and driving

- To set curfews

- To tell guests possessing drugs to leave the youth activity and not to return

Today PACK is still a live and viable organization, helping children and teens in their efforts to become educated, healthy, and responsible adults. Under the capable leadership of President Sue Busse, representatives from every public school in the district attend the meetings as liaison persons. They plan their own school's drug-prevention efforts. Each school contributes financially to PACK through the PTO Board. Also involved in the meetings are the local Juvenile Officer, a representative from the Kirkwood Youth Advisory Council, and interested citizens.

While PACK was gathering steam, Kirkwood High School began its attack on the drug problem. Most of the preventative efforts that school officials started then continue to the present time. During the 1984-1985 school year, the Student Assistance Team, composed of counselors, teachers, administrators, the school nurse, and consultants, was formed to help identify troubled students. They targeted such problems as student drug use, eating disorders, and physical, emotional, and sexual abuse. The team exists at present. Once a referral is made regarding a student, the team jumps in to assess the problem and to secure help for the student. Ken Finnerty, a high school counselor, is the Student Assistance Team Coordinator. The team meets weekly to evaluate each student referred and to recommend strategies.

A SADD group (Students Against Driving Drunk) also exists at the high school to promote awareness of the dangers involved in drinking and driving. The students themselves organized and currently promote TREND (Turning Recreational Excitement in New Directions) activities and plan their own substance-free activities. The group's message is "Celebrate Sober."

The COPE support group is directed at the needs of students who come from chemically-dependent families. Another group called SUPPORT gives help to those students who are themselves chemically dependent and who have been through a treatment or recovery program. (Experience has shown that without strong support, students tend to return to their addictions.)

Students involve themselves in Red Ribbon Week (a local, state, and national drug-awareness week). They dispense red ribbons and paint grocery bags with anti-drug slogans, which they distribute to local supermarkets. (Middle and grade school students participate also.) The school also sponsors Awareness Week, a biennial event involving speakers and resource groups who talk with students on drug-abuse prevention topics.

The high school also has in existence the Peer Helper program. Its focus is to identify students who are "natural helpers" and then train them to listen to their peers who are troubled or seeking assistance. The middle schools call their "natural helpers" program —"Friends Assisting Friends." The high school has also initiated "walking counselors"—adults who walk the halls to listen to the problems the students wish to share with them. While teachers and administrators are busy at their tasks, the counselors also make sure school rules are followed.

While the community was struggling with its problems, a young man named Keith Rawlings was struggling with problems of his own. He recounts the events that brought them about.

While attending college in North Dakota, I started a puppet ministry with my friend, Tim. We traveled to places no one else wanted to go. We felt the children of poor communities needed a spiritual message, too. We set up a non-profit corporation. When we were not in class, we traveled all over the United States and Canada. We did not charge a fee because we felt that people would give what they could. Unfortunately, the debts were larger than the free-will offerings we received.

After college, Tim and I accepted a call to a large church in Atlanta where we served as Youth Ministers for the Children's

Youth Ministry Program. After eight months, however, the church decided to make budget cuts and the children's programs were cut back to almost nothing. The minister told us that we would be out of a job in two weeks. I had no idea what I would do next. I didn't have any savings because all the extra money had gone to our puppet ministry. I finally called home and asked my mom if I could come to St. Louis.

This was the biggest setback I had ever faced. My self-esteem was pretty low. I could hardly face my family and friends. I had been gone for several years, but I thought I could get my old job back. I went in to apply only to find out that there were no immediate openings. Later, I accepted a position at a fast-food restaurant as Store Activities Representative. The job helped to pay the immediate bills for the puppet ministry. I contacted an attorney. He agreed to help me free of charge. He said my only option was to file bankruptcy for the puppet ministry and also for myself, since I had put a lot of the ministry's expenses on my credit cards.

With the doom and gloom of bankruptcy over my head, I set out to concentrate on my interest in helping youth. I took a volunteer position as a youth director in a local church. At the fast-food restaurant, I met a young lady who worked the breakfast and lunch shifts and attended college in the afternoon and evening. We started dating and soon fell in love. I proposed to her, and she accepted.

Lisa and I held a common interest in youth. We were aware of the pressures kids had with alcohol and other drugs. There seemed to be a lack of supervised activities for the kids in our community. We agreed something had to be done. We set out to develop a non-profit corporation designed to teach and protect the youth in our area. In 1986 we founded the Kirkwood Youth Advisory Council (YAC). It was a part of my recovery from discouragement.

The Council has been very successful in its short life of seven years. With the founding of YAC, a coalition was formed that includes representatives from service clubs, the local police department, the city council, the local hospital, business and community leaders, juvenile court, parents, local task forces, and the Chamber of Commerce. The Council meets once a month to plan activities and to keep informed of drug problems in the neighborhood.

At its inception, the coalition decided to target youth in the middle schools. It sponsors safe and drug-free activities and an environment in which to gather and have fun. Activities have included:

•Skateboard jams—a local radio station provides safety tips, skill stations, and videos for skateboard safety

•Bicycle Safety Awareness Days—includes safety tips and inspections, trail rides and riding demonstrations

•Bake sales—provided by Council members and volunteers for community functions, along with YAC promotion

•Theme dances—the youth enjoy dancing to top tunes and munching on their favorite "junk" foods. Often those attending are asked to bring canned goods for needy families

•Dive-In movies—the youth bring their own innertubes or rafts to a local pool to watch a movie on a large screen

•Youth Awareness Days—days of workshops benefitting teens and parents

•Participation in the local Greentree Festival and parade—the Council provides games for children, a float in the parade and an information booth

•Elf Workshops—while parents Christmas shop, children make crafts and wrap them as Christmas gifts for family members

•Scavenger hunts—youth ask for donations of food and staples for the needy

•Slide presentations—showing two and a half years of fun-filled activities sponsored by the Council

Other projects of the organization include:

•A mentor program that takes local high school students into community businesses to work part-time in their chosen fields

•A Youth Recognition Award, which is given to those youths in the area making outstanding contributions

•A Youth Survey, which is presented to the city at a general meeting

•An area youth directory, which has been compiled, promoting YAC and containing a list of phone numbers of "help" agencies in the area. Ten thousand directories were distributed in one year.

•A program in which parents chaperone youth activities and volunteer for baking, folding, and publicity for the Council

On October 4, 1989, the Council received a proclamation from Missouri Governor John Ashcroft, recognizing the third anniversary of its founding. It also received an award from the Missouri Federation of Parents for Drug-Free Youth for dedicated service.

YAC also sponsors a Junior Council consisting of youth from the sixth, seventh, and eighth grades. This group helps plan and organize activities for its peers. It gives aid to senior citizens and shut-ins. The Junior Council also publishes and circulates a youth newspaper, *The Yacker*, containing news articles, upcoming events, and special interest stories pertinent to youth.

As Keith Rawlings says, "Basically we wanted the youth involved and off the streets. 'There's nothing to do' has always been their famous complaint."

In 1987, the city received another "boost" when Mrs. Nell Bishop, a local citizen, was elected President of the Missouri Federation of Parents for Drug-Free Youth. Her tireless efforts brought the city into focus with the state organization.

By 1988, the community had truly begun to survive the drug war and to fight back! In that year, the Kirkwood School District R-7 launched its Drug-Free Schools Program, citing many goals and objectives. Among those goals was their intention to identify students most at risk for substance abuse in dysfunctional families and to encourage those to seek counseling.

During the 1988-1989 school year, the Missouri Drug-Free Schools and Community Grant paved the way for an even bigger thrust in the community war on drugs. Believing that families are the first line of defense against substance abuse, the school district, with the help of the grant, greatly increased its efforts to provide prevention activities, educational opportunities, and support services. Programs were implemented in both public and non-public schools.

A school district Advisory Committee was set up, consisting of representatives from local law-enforcement agencies, civic leaders, full-time counselors, nurses, parents, students, and teachers and administrators from each of the schools. Under the leadership of Vern Beckmann, who at that time was Director of student services for the district, each school was asked to appoint its own prevention team and to set its own goals and strategies for that school.

This program continues to the present.

Successful Parenting classes were also begun because of an expressed need on the part of parents to sharpen their parenting skills and provide support.

DARE (Drug Abuse Resistance Education) was begun—a 17-week program in which local, trained, uniformed police officers teach resistance skills to 5th graders at school. It was initiated as a cooperative effort between the police department and the school district.

At the invitation of the school district, Sharon Scott, a licensed professional counselor, consultant, and author, spoke to 400 parents on the topic of "Peer Pressure Reversal" and conducted a workshop for 98 staff members. At present, the Kirkwood school district counselors have a resource library composed of books, pamphlets, and videos related to chemical dependency. The materials are available for loan to citizens.

A newsletter, *Connections*, is mailed three times a year to every student's home. It strives to educate parents on prevention issues and related topics.

It was also decided that the Drug-Free Schools Grant would pay for a local counseling agency to provide counseling sessions with high-risk students and their families. Progressive Youth Center, a United Way not-for-profit agency, was the counseling agency chosen to provide the service. All of the counseling is related to potential substance abuse by any family member. School counselors, nurses, and teachers identify families needing agency help. The first year, approximately 80 non-coping families received counseling. The service provides the first three counseling sessions at no cost to the family. In addition, the Drug-Free School Advisory Committee conducts an assessment of the schools' drug problems every three years in grades seven and twelve. This survey identifies areas needing attention.

Dr. Beckmann said, "I believe the student surveys indicate that there is a decline in the use of hard drugs, although alcohol is still a problem. The family counseling program has had a strong, positive impact on students and families."

Dr. Beckmann retired in 1991. His successor, Michael Eldridge, says of the Drug-Free Schools Program:

The importance of our Drug-Free Schools Program cannot be overstated. Although it is not what would be considered a part of our basic curriculum, its learning activities are designed to provide students with information and skills that should have a positive influence on their present and future lifestyles.

I believe we are fighting a war against drugs that has rapidly spread throughout our society. In Kirkwood, our volunteer army of educators, parents, and community representatives has taken an early offensive. I hope our battle cry will be, "Make Kirkwood children drug free."

In 1991, the Kirkwood School District was recognized by the National Prevention Network in Washington, D.C. as one of the top fifty percent of communities in the nation with exemplary programs for drug prevention.

In spite of the honor, seventy-one percent of twelfth-grade students disclosed that they had held or attended parties where an adult chaperone was seldom or never present. "Keg" parties had also become a big problem in the neighborhood. Principal McCallie of Kirkwood High School further said:

Between 1987 and 1989, we became aware that the students were talking about many more alcohol parties in the community involving heavy alcohol usage. The students themselves were reporting that 200-300 kids were at a particular student's home on a given night for a party and they were describing the behavior of other kids at the parties.

Because of their concern, high school parents Ron and Frances Hall, in conjunction with the high school PTO Executive Committee, began the Parent Network group. The Network involves parents and keeps them informed of problems. "Safe homes" are designated. (Participating parents agree to sign a pledge stating that parties held in their homes will be "safe"—chaperoned and substance-free). For the information of other parents, their pledge is acknowledged by an asterisk after their names in the "buzz book" published by each school. (The book is a school information booklet containing the names and addresses of all students' parents). The "Safe homes" concept has been adopted also in middle schools.

A *Parent to Parent* handbook is also distributed in which parents are advised to:

- Welcome communication from other parents; get to know their children's friends and their parents
- Communicate with other parents regarding teen activities in the community.
- Leave a responsible adult in charge when they (the parents) are out of town.
- Check with parents of their children's friends before parties and overnights to insure that the activity will be chaperoned and drug-free.
- Be awake or awakened when young people come home at night.
- Assure their teens they can call to be picked up at any time.
- Refrain from allowing parties or gatherings in the home when they (the parents) are not present.

The community has learned a lesson—it takes an *entire* community's efforts to fight the drug problem, and the efforts must be continuous!

One citizen deals with the problem constantly. Geoff Morrison has been Kirkwood's Juvenile Officer since 1979. Teens call him "Clark Kent." Indeed, he fits the picture. He is truly one of the "super men" in the whole drug-prevention picture. In spite of a heavy case-load, Geoff still finds time to attend many drug-prevention meetings. He is also the liaison between the police department and the district.

Jeannie Webdell is the city's Crime Prevention Officer. It is her responsibility to work with the Community Crime Watch program, Night-Out Against Crime (when citizens gather to promote crime prevention in their neighborhoods), and to foster and change social attitudes.

In a 1987 Youth Advisory Council survey of the teen community, 90 percent of the youth between the ages of 12 and 18 believed there were not enough activities offered for them. In 1989, another YAC survey of 1,103 teens in the city showed that the biggest problem among the youth was a lack of recreational facilities.

In 1991, fourteen-year-old Susan Brown wrote:

Where to Go?

In Kirkwood there are no places to go for teenagers. The only place there is to go is the ice rink where you can't just go and talk, you have to skate or you get thrown out. Other places are the streets or the park and you can't go there at night to talk without being thrown out. The places teenagers go are to other friends' houses, which usually lead to parties and parties lead to alcohol and drugs. Why won't Kirkwood set up a place to go for teenagers? . . .

Why are teenagers being pushed out of Kirkwood? I think Kirkwood kids would like to see a place where 13-18 year olds can go eat, listen to music and have fun, without people saying, "Get out" or "Don't come in."

Kids in Kirkwood usually go to malls, and people make trouble at Crestwood or Galleria and fool around. Even in the malls we can't sit at a table to talk without buying food. Everyone is telling us to get out. Where are we supposed to go? You tell us!

Susan has targeted the problem. Now the dream of local citizens is for a teen center—a "nice hangout" in which the youth of the community could gather. Another dream is a temporary youth shelter, where a youth in trouble could stay for a short time in safety until better solutions to his problems are found.

In October, 1990, a survey of seniors at Kirkwood High School showed a definite drop in the number of drug abusers and in the frequency of drug abuse after the Drug-Free Schools Program had been in place for two years. In spite of all the communities' drug prevention efforts, a 1991 survey showed that 61.5 percent of the seniors had used alcohol within the past month. Forty-three percent of the group reported having had five or more drinks in a row within the last two weeks. Clearly, alcohol was found to be the drug of choice of students in the community. That choice continues to the present.

Furthermore, in a 1992 report from the Missouri Department of Health, seventh and twelfth graders continue to rate alcohol as the most commonly abused drug in the United States in their age groups. On the contrary, a National Council on Alcoholism report of high school seniors nationwide showed that marijuana use "within the last 30 days," dropped from 37 percent in 1979 to only 14 percent in 1990.

Pam Hughes, guidance counselor at Kirkwood High School and member of the Missouri Drug-Free Schools Advisory Committee, makes this observation:

> I agree with author Anne Wilson Schaef that we are basically an addictive society. Given that fact, it is no surprise that our children are having problems with a variety of kinds of addictions. And, given the degree to which alcohol use is accepted within our society, it is especially no surprise that our children view alcohol use in a casual way.
>
> Part of the solution is going to require not only developing programs that are targeted at our children, but programs that will help change the attitudes of society as a whole and which get at the root of the problem. Getting at the root involves building self-esteem, finding meaning in one's work and one's life, developing methods of problem-solving, and finding ways of belonging. When we try to solve community problems, it's important to go beyond dealing with the symptoms and try to look more systemically at the root causes.

To complicate the city's problem further, through the years, Kirkwood citizens learned that their comparatively peaceful, quiet community was not immune to violence. Three drug "incidents" happened that further alerted citizens to the dangers.

In December, 1990, a St. Louis teenager was shot and killed on South Harrison Street in Kirkwood, after being abducted and held until an associate could deliver money from drug sales. When the companion escaped, the youth was shot and his body left on the street. Three teenagers were later arrested and convicted in court for the abduction/slaying.

Furthermore, in June, 1991, a three-year-old girl and an 18-month-old-boy were taken into protective custody after an anonymous report that their mother had let them wander around the neighborhood. After police arrived at the house, the children were taken into custody when officers found the mother to be incoherent and unsteady on her feet. She admitted to juvenile court authorities that she had been using cocaine. She voluntarily accepted drug treatment and her children were eventually returned to her.

In addition, in October, 1992, a young man who had had only minor problems with the law was arrested after robbing a delicatessen employee in the city at knifepoint. He pleaded guilty to armed robbery and was sentenced to six years in prison. He reportedly had a cocaine habit at the time of the robbery and had to resort to the crime to obtain money for drugs.

In view of incidents such as these, Herb Jones, mayor of Kirkwood from 1984 to 1992, made his drug program a city priority. He provided the leadership for the city to adopt a strategic plan of action. His planning group initiated the idea of the "Buck Drugs" program. Citizens were asked to give one "buck" or more to provide funds to people who give information leading to an arrest or the solution of a crime. (The lack of investigative leads about drug sales and unsolved crimes were seen as major problems.) An information hot line number was set up. The "Buck Drugs" program is on-going and has led to arrests. A drug-abuse policy for city employees was also established as a part of Mayor Jones' strategy.

Additionally, scholarships allow high-risk children in grades one through five to attend summer day camps where part of the focus is drug-abuse resistance. The six-week camp is sponsored jointly by the Department of Recreation and the Police Department. Scholarships are provided through a grant from the Missouri Department of Mental Health. DARE officers play a significant role in the camp.

The city's present mayor, Marge Schramm, makes this observation of the drug-prevention efforts of the last ten years:

> Kirkwood groups have taken a variety of approaches to the drug and alcohol problems facing the community. We have been particularly proud of leadership by police and recreation departments working with schools and other community groups.
>
> As well, the Southeast Kirkwood neighborhood of Meacham Park has been chosen as one of nine St. Louis city and county neighborhoods to participate in the Prevention Partnership. Funded by a grant from the Office of Substance Abuse, the partnership will work on drug and alcohol problems.
>
> With the help of the Prevention Partnership staff, community leaders in southeast Kirkwood will work to develop resources and to design, implement, and maintain their own projects to meet the goals of the grant.

The community has come a long way since its first efforts in the fall of 1983. It still has a long way to go. But, it has proven that a community, by its own best efforts, can survive the drug war, and make great strides in eliminating the problem that plagues almost all of America's cities.